ALAIN ON HAPPINESS

Alain

ALAIN ON HAPPINESS

Translated by Robert D. and
Jane E. Cottrell

Introduction by Robert D. Cottrell

FREDERICK UNGAR PUBLISHING CO.
NEW YORK

Translated from the original French, *Propos sur le bonheur,*
by arrangement with Editions Gallimard, Paris. Copyright by
Editions Gallimard 1928

Copyright © 1973 by Frederick Ungar Publishing Co., Inc.
Printed in the United States of America
Designed by Paula Wiener
Library of Congress Catalog Card Number: 76-186356
ISBN: 0-8044-5033-1

Some few of us realize that in a hundred years Alain's writings will be more widely appreciated than works which are today considered classics.

I was happy recently when an American professor of philosophy said to me: "Do you know that France is the home of a great man who is comparatively unknown, an essayist who writes under the name of Alain?"

"He is far from unknown," I said. "He is known among those who are worthy of knowing him!"

André Maurois

Contents

✿ vii

Contents

Contents

Contents

x *

Introduction

When he died in 1951 at the age of eighty-three, Emile Chartier, the brilliant philosophy professor who had published numerous books and thousands of articles under the pseudonym of Alain, had been loved and revered by several generations of Frenchmen. He had left an indelible mark on the minds and lives of not only his most gifted pupils, including André Maurois, Simone Weil, and Maurice Schumann, but on all who had had the good fortune to attend his classes. Like any great teacher, Chartier taught more than books. He instilled in his many pupils a love for truth, a sense of hope, and the firm conviction that they could fashion their own future. Robust, frank, and generous, he won the admiration and lasting devotion of his students who often called him, with eloquent simplicity, *l'Homme*—The Man.

For us of a different language and of a later generation it is not Chartier the teacher we know, but Alain the writer. Of course, the philosophy teacher and the writer were inseparable. Alain aimed, as he said, to change philosophy into literature and literature into philosophy. Like the sixteenth-century essayist Montaigne, who maintained that "there is

Introduction

nothing more joyful, more jovial, more lighthearted, and I might almost say more playful" than philosophy, Alain wished to free men from fear and "to cleanse this world of all the human vapors" that cloud our perceptions. Opposed to any form of dogmatism and to tyranny, whether of the body or the mind, he constantly displayed a strong streak of practicality and common sense typical of the Norman peasants who were his ancestors.

Born in 1868, Alain was the son of a successful veterinarian. A brilliantly gifted student, he could have elected a career in medicine, science, music, or any of a dozen other professions. He chose instead to study philosophy and literature at the *Ecole Normale*, the most rigorous and glorious of French institutions of higher learning. After earning his degree in 1892, he began teaching, first at Pontivy and then at Lorient. In 1894 the Dreyfus Affair bitterly divided French public opinion. Alain, who was fervently interested in politics and incensed at the treatment accorded Dreyfus, wrote a series of articles for a radical newspaper, *La Dépêche de Lorient*, defending Dreyfus and exposing the hypocrisies and duplicities of Dreyfus' accusers. During the next ten years he pursued his teaching career, engaged from time to time in political and journalistic activity, and published numerous articles on philosophical topics as well as a book-length study on Spinoza.

From 1900 to 1902 Alain taught at Rouen, and although he moved to Paris in 1903, his friends in Rouen convinced him to contribute articles to a local newspaper. Beginning in 1903 *La Dépêche de Rouen* carried a rather long weekly article by Alain.

Every writer discovers by trial and error the rhythm and pace that suit him best. Alain, whose thought is incisive and tends to be aphoristic, felt ill-at-ease writing a column of considerable length. "Those articles poisoned my whole week," he later noted in his memoirs. For some three years, however, he doggedly continued to write his weekly column. Then, early in 1906 he decided to try writing a short article every day instead of a longer one each week; "that would permit me to make amends immediately for a botched article."

These shorter articles began appearing in the same newspaper, *La Dépêche de Rouen*, on February 16, 1906, eleven days after the demise of the longer column. The title of the new daily column was *Propos d'un Normand*; it was signed simply "Alain," the pseudonym Emile Chartier had derived from the name of the fifteenth-century Norman poet, Alain Chartier. From 1906 until the outbreak of World War I, Alain continued to write a two-page article each evening, changing philosophy not only into literature, but into journalism as well. By 1914 he had published 3,078 such articles, which he called *propos* (remarks). After the war he wrote some 2,000 additional *propos* for various newspapers and magazines, but never again did he adhere to the schedule of one a day. However, he was by then writing books as well as *propos*, and for the next thirty years scarcely a year passed without the publication of one or more of Alain's remarkable books on philosophy, politics, esthetics, or literature. His fame as a writer was soon firmly established.

From time to time some of the *propos* were rescued from that limbo to which most journalism is consigned, and were published in book form. Out of the mass of nearly 5,000 *propos*, editors chose to collect and publish in individual volumes those that dealt with one particular subject. Thus, in 1928 ninety-three *propos* dealing with the general theme of happiness were published under the title of *Propos sur le bonheur*.

The word *propos*, as Alain used it, is virtually untranslatable.

* xiii

Introduction

Montaigne, to whom Alain has frequently been compared, had used a common noun, *essai*, or essay, meaning trial or test, to define what it was that he was writing, and the word soon came to denote a particular literary genre whose distinctive characteristics were those of an essay by Montaigne. Similarly, Alain used the common noun, *propos*, a word rich in meanings, to define his newspaper articles; in so doing he created a unique literary genre as distinctive as the essay Montaigne had created. Basically, the French word *propos* means spoken words, or words exchanged in the course of a conversation. It therefore suggests something relatively informal and social. Furthermore, it contains the notion of proposing; Alain's *propos* are propositions which the reader is invited, and indeed urged, to examine. The overlapping meanings of the word itself indicate in a general way the rhythm and tonality of Alain's *propos*. Short aphoristic pieces of fifty or sixty lines, they move along easily and wittily.

Alain made it a principle never to rewrite or modify what he had once written down. Years later he recalled how he wrote the *propos*: each evening he would sit down before two sheets of paper, knowing before he started that the last line would be written on the bottom of the second page, and that within the confines of those two pages he would write a piece which, if he succeeded, would have "movement, air, and elevation." He also knew that he would make no corrections, erasures, or changes; since the piece would be published the next day, he did not have time for the niceties of anguished composition. He saw the bottom of the second page approach, and ruthlessly suppressed every idea that was not germane to his theme. "The final barrier approached as other ideas began to appear; they were repressed; but, and I don't know how, they succeeded in filling out the principal idea. . . . The result was a kind of poetry and strength."

The urgent necessity of meeting a journalistic deadline taught Alain another lesson: he learned the importance of exercising the will. There is, he realized, only one way for a man to create anything, whether it be the writing of an article, the making of a chair, or the planting of a garden, and that is simply to do it. Here we approach the heart of Alain's message on happiness: there is no happiness except what a man creates for himself by exercising his will. "Certainly we do not become what we want to become," he wrote in an article entitled "Comments on the Art of Knowing Others and Oneself"; "but we do not become anything at all if first we do not exercise our will." And the ninetieth *propos* on happiness begins with the assertion: "We must will to be happy, and work at it." The very discipline required in the composition of the *propos* gave Alain an opportunity to exercise his will. A product of the will, the *propos* on happiness are a series of richly embroidered variations on the theme of judicious use of the will.

But in order to exercise one's will wisely and to procure the maximum happiness from life while suffering only the minimum amount of unhappiness, one must first perceive the causes of both happiness and unhappiness, of joy and sadness. In short, one must be able to perceive reality clearly. Indeed, Alain devoted the first three months of his famous philosophy courses to lectures on perception. A similar approach may be seen in the *propos*.

A *propos* by Alain nearly always begins with a reference to something precise and immediately recognizable. Sometimes it is an incident familiar to all his readers, such as the sinking of the *Titanic* (*Propos* XIV); sometimes it is a personal anecdote (as in *Propos* XXVII); often it is a reference to those activities of the human body with which we are all familiar—sneezing, coughing, yawning, scratching, or swallowing.

The first *propos* in *Alain on Happiness* is not only typical of

Introduction

Alain's style but also contains the major themes that will be treated with considerable virtuosity throughout the entire book. It opens with the evocation of a crying baby; his nurse, trying to determine the cause of the infant's distress, imagines numerous fanciful causes to explain the very audible effect. Finally, she perceives the obvious, that a pin is the real cause of the trouble. Alain, not content with this homey anecdote illustrating the futility of abstract speculation when detached from the reality of the concrete world, then relates another story illustrating the same theme. This time, however, the story is remote in time and place; it is the legendary account of how young Alexander tamed the untameable horse, Bucephalus.

Although Alain's *propos* are firmly rooted in physical reality, they often bear, lightly and even gaily, a rich cargo of legend, myth, philosophy, and literature. Alexander, of course, perceived that Bucephalus was afraid of his own shadow, and, turning the horse's head toward the sun, managed to calm him and then to train him. "We have no power at all over our passions as long as we do not know their true causes," declares Alain, restating in slightly extended form the conclusion he had reached at the end of the first anecdote. The *propos* then moves from the specific to the general. The body of the article is devoted to a series of remarks and observations suggested to the author by the two stories he has just related. Like leitmotifs, the words crying, fear, and pin reappear in various guises. Comments and reflections which, in the work of another writer, might well serve as a springboard for speculation, are constantly checked and brought back to the real world by concrete examples that are artfully spaced throughout the *propos*. Thus, in a brief sentence Alain rapidly relates a comic incident in the life of Marshal Masséna; in the following paragraph he refers to a remark of Talleyrand; several sentences later he evokes "the evils of 1914."

The central part, or development section, of a *propos* is not constructed like a philosophical demonstration, one idea leading logically and irrefutably to another. Instead, Alain's remarks circle around the single idea which was contained in the opening sentences. They spiral around the basic theme, illuminating it from unexpected angles. The tone is alert, relaxed, and friendly. The conclusion, which is usually a succinct final sentence, pointing, like a fable or a parable, to a practical lesson, often takes the reader by surprise. It is nearly always pungent. Generally, it returns the reader to the familiar world of common experience which had been evoked at the beginning of the *propos*. Often, as in the first *propos*, it brings him back abruptly to the initial incident. "Look for the pin," concludes *Propos* I, but now the word "pin" is laden with all the metaphorical meanings that have accrued to it throughout the course of the *propos*.

Agreeing with the Stoics, with Descartes, and with Spinoza, "that master of contentment," as he called him, Alain affirms that, except for real physical pain and the few genuine misfortunes that befall us only infrequently, our unhappiness is caused by our passions, which in turn are nurtured by our thoughts and imagination. Fear, despair, anger, irritation, in a word, all our passions alter the functioning of our body. The muscles become tense, the heart beats faster, and breathing becomes difficult. "Still, our passions can be managed," declares Alain. Not easily, however, and not without an understanding of the relationship between our thoughts and our body. We are not free to control our thoughts directly, nor are we able to rid ourselves of the passions that promote unhappiness by simply wanting to. We can, however, control our bodily movements. "Man's will has no control over his passions, but does have direct control over his movements." And direct control over our movements is precisely the means whereby we can indirectly control our passions. For, and this is the wise man's secret which was first demonstrated by Descartes, the passions are not autonomous; they are in fact dependent upon the movements of the body. "A man who is bored," writes Alain, "has a way of sitting down, of getting up, of speaking, which is calculated to promote boredom." Therefore the only way to counteract our passions is by governing the body; in short, by judicious action.

To illustrate his concept of action as an indirect control of the passions, Alain introduces the notion of gymnastics. "Once accustomed to doing certain things, once the muscles are trained and exercised by gymnastics, we can act as we wish." Thus, he points out the powerful effects that posture, ritual, politeness, and ceremonies can have in controlling passions and in creating happiness. For happiness must be created. Joy must be cultivated. In a world that is neither hostile nor friendly, there is nothing favorable to man except what he makes through his own efforts.

One of Alain's favorite myths, referred to twice in *Alain on Happiness*, is the myth of Er which Plato relates in the closing pages of *The Republic*. Er, who had been thought dead, descended to Hades, and when the error was discovered, returned to earth where he told his friends what he had seen down there. The souls, explained Er, were given the choice of a new destiny. Still remembering their past life, they chose according to their desires and regrets. Each soul then took his destiny, drank of the river of Forgetfulness, and returned to earth to live as he had chosen. Whether our destiny be happiness or unhappiness, Alain suggests, is largely a matter of our own choice. "We must stand firm," he once wrote, "between two kinds of madness: the belief that we can do anything; and the belief that we can do nothing." Alain's work is an act of faith in the human spirit. It dispels fear, and fosters hope. When old and severely crippled by arthritis, Alain looked back over his long life, his numerous works, and wrote with the serene confidence that characterized him: "There is a way of singing which shows that one is not afraid, and which reassures the world of men."

ROBERT D. COTTRELL

I

Bucephalus

When a baby cries and refuses to be consoled, his nurse often makes the most ingenious suppositions about his character and his likes and dislikes. She even resorts to heredity for explanations, and can already recognize the father in his son. These attempts at psychology continue until the nurse discovers the pin, the real cause of the trouble.

When Bucephalus, the famous horse, was presented to young Alexander, not a single equerry could ride the fierce animal. An ordinary man might have said: "There's a mean horse if I ever saw one." Alexander, however, began to look for the pin, and soon found it when he noticed that Bucephalus was terribly afraid of his own shadow. Since his fear also made his shadow buck, it was a vicious circle. But Alexander turned Bucephalus' head toward the sun and, keeping him turned that way, managed to calm him and then to break him in. Thus Aristotle's pupil already realized that we have no power at all over our passions as long as we do not know their true causes.

Many men have refuted fear, and with sound arguments. But a man who is afraid does not listen to arguments; he listens to the beating of his heart and the pulsating of his blood. The pedant's reasoning proceeds from danger to fear; the reasoning of a man who is governed by his passions proceeds from fear to danger. Both are trying to be logical, and both are mistaken. The pedant, however, is doubly mistaken; he does not know the real cause and does not understand the passionate man's error. A man who is afraid invents a danger in order to explain his fear, which is real and quite apparent. The least surprise arouses fear even if there is no danger at all, as for example, an unexpected pistol shot nearby, or simply the presence of an unexpected person. Marshal Masséna was once frightened by a statue on a dimly lighted staircase, and ran for his life.

Impatience and ill humor sometimes result from the fact that a man has been on his feet too long. Do not try to reason him out of his ill humor; offer him a chair. When Talleyrand said that manners are everything, he said more than he realized. In the care he took to be accommodating, he was looking for the pin, and always ended up by finding it. All of today's diplomats have a misplaced pin somewhere in their breeches; hence Europe's problems. We all know that one squalling child makes others cry. And worse still, crying makes one cry even harder. With professional competence, a nurse turns the infant over on his stomach. Soon there are different responses and a different pattern of behavior. Now there is a down-to-earth method of persuasion. In my opinion, the evils of 1914 resulted from all the important men being surprised; consequently, they were overcome by fear. When a man is afraid, he is not very far from anger; irritation follows agitation. It is not a favorable situation when a man is brusquely called away from his leisure and repose; often he changes, and changes too much. Like a man awakened by surprise; he wakes up too much. But never say that men are wicked; never say that they are of such and such a character. Look for the pin.

8 December 1922

II

Irritation

When you swallow wrong, a great tumult occurs in the body, as if an imminent danger were being announced to all its parts. Each of the muscles reacts in its own way, including the heart; it is a kind of convulsion. What can we do about it? Are we able to restrain ourselves and avoid succumbing to all these reactions? That is what the philosopher will say, because he is a man without experience. But a gymnast or a fencing instructor would certainly laugh if his pupil said: "I can't help it; I can't stop myself from tightening up and tensing all my muscles." I once knew a harsh man who, after asking for permission, would vigorously lash out at you with his foil in order to open up the paths to reason. Here is a well-known fact: the muscles naturally follow along after thoughts, like docile dogs. I think about stretching out my arm, and soon afterwards I stretch it out. The principal cause of these convulsions and upheavals I was talking about a moment ago is precisely that we do not know what to do about them. And, in the above example, what you should do is relax the whole body; more particularly, instead of inhaling forcibly, which aggravates the condition, you should expel the few drops of liquid which have gone down the wrong way. In other words, it comes down to driving out fear which, in this case as in all others, is totally harmful.

As for the cough which accompanies a cold, there is a similar kind of discipline, too infrequently practiced. Most people cough in the same way they scratch themselves, with a kind of fury of which they are the victims. This results in exhausting and irritating paroxysms. As a remedy, doctors have hit on lozenges, whose principal function is, I believe, to make us swallow. Swallowing is a powerful reaction, even less voluntary than coughing, even further outside of our control. The convulsion of swallowing makes impossible that other convulsion which results in coughing. Once again it is a matter of turning the baby over. But I believe that if, in the first moment, one could avoid the tragic stance inherent in a cough, then one could do without lozenges. If, without any ado, one remained relaxed and imperturbable at the outset, the first irritation would soon pass.

This word, irritation, ought to make us think. Through the wisdom of language, it is also used to designate the most violent of passions. Indeed, I do not see much difference between a man who gives himself up to anger and one who abandons himself to a fit of coughing. Similarly, fear is an anguish of the body which we do not always know how to combat with gymnastics. In all these cases, the mistake is to place thought at the service of passions and to throw oneself into fear or anger with a kind of wild enthusiasm. In short, we aggravate our malady with our passions. Such is the destiny of those who have not learned true gymnastics. And true gymnastics, as the Greeks realized, is the sovereignty of clear reason over the movements of the body. Not over all of them, of course. But it is simply a question of not hindering natural reactions by frenzied movements. And, in my opinion, that is what children should be taught, by suggesting that they always take as models the most beautiful statues, objects worthy of human devotion.

5 December 1912

III

Sad Mary

It is not futile to reflect on cycles of depression and elation, and notably on that "Sad Mary-Joyful Mary" whom one of our psychologists was fortunate enough to find in his clinic. The story, already nearly forgotten, is worth recalling. This girl was happy one week and sad the next, with the regularity of a clock. When she was happy, everything went well; she liked the rain as well as the sun; she went into raptures at the slightest indications of friendship; when she thought about one of her male friends, she would say: "How lucky I am!" She never got bored; her most trifling thoughts were tinged with joy, like beautiful flowers, flourishing and lovely. She was in that state which I wish for you, my friends. For every amphora, as the wise man says, has two handles; similarly, every event has two sides, calamitous if one so wishes, comforting and consoling if one wishes. And the effort we make to be happy is never lost.

But after a week, the tune changed. She fell into a hopeless languor; nothing interested her any more; her glance withered everything. She no longer believed in happiness; she no longer believed in love. No one had ever loved her; and everyone was

6 *

perfectly justified in not doing so; she thought of herself as stupid and boring; she aggravated her distress by thinking about it, and she knew she was doing it; she tore herself to shreds with a kind of horrible thoroughness. She would say: "You want to make me think that you're interested in me, but you can't fool me." A compliment would be a way of making fun of her; a kindness, a way of humiliating her. A secret would be a very sinister plot. These imagined torments are without remedy, in the sense that the most felicitous events smile in vain on the man who is unhappy. And will power is a greater factor in happiness than one might think.

But the psychologist was to discover an even harsher truth, a more formidable trial for a courageous spirit. In the course of his many observations and analyses of these brief human seasons, he happened to include a blood count. And the law was revealed. Toward the end of a happy period, the number of red blood cells diminished; toward the end of a sad period, they began to increase. Deficiency and richness of the blood— that was the cause of all this phantasmagoria of the imagination. Thus the doctor was in a position to answer Mary's emotional entreaties: "Don't worry about it; tomorrow you will be happy." But she refused to believe anything of the kind.

A friend of mine who likes to think of himself as being fundamentally sad said to me about this story: "What could be plainer than that? We can't do anything about it. I can't acquire more blood cells simply by wishing. Therefore, all philosophy is futile. This vast universe will bring us joy or sadness, according to its own laws, just like winter and summer, rain and sunshine. My desire to be happy carries no more weight than my desire to go for a walk; I don't make the rain fall on this valley; I don't make the melancholy that is within me. I bear it, and I know that I am bearing it. Some consolation!"

*

7

It is not that simple. It is clear that in mulling over harsh judgments, sinister predictions, and bad memories, we fashion our own sadness; in a certain sense, we savor it. But if I know that underneath it all it is a question of blood cells, I can laugh at my speculations; I can thrust my sadness back into my body, where it is no longer anything but fatigue or illness— nothing fancier. A stomach ache is easier to bear than a betrayal. And is it not better to say that you are deficient in blood cells, rather than in true friends? The emotional man rejects explanations as well as calmatives. Is it not remarkable that by the method I have indicated the doors to both these remedies are opened at the same time?

18 August 1913

IV

Neurasthenia

During periods of sudden storms, the moods of men, and women, too, are as changeable as the skies. A friend of mine who is very knowledgeable and quite sensible was telling me yesterday: "I'm not satisfied with myself. As soon as I stop working or am not playing bridge, a hundred little scraps of thought go round in my head, making me sad one minute, happy the next, and with a hundred little variations, faster than a chameleon changes color. These scraps of thought—a letter to be written, a streetcar I missed, or a topcoat that is too heavy—take on extraordinary importance, as if they were genuine misfortunes. In vain I try to reason with myself and prove to myself that these things shouldn't upset me. My arguments sound no more impressive to me than soggy drums. In short, I'm feeling a bit neurasthenic."

Stop using big words, I told him, and try to see things as they are. Your lot is no different from that of everybody else; it is just that you have the misfortune of being intelligent, of thinking too much about yourself, and of wanting to understand why you are sad one minute and happy the next. And you get annoyed with yourself because you can't identify the causes of either your joy or your sadness.

As a matter of fact, specific reasons for happiness or unhappiness do not really count; everything depends on our body and its functions. The most robust organism alternates many times each day between tension and listlessness, listlessness and tension, influenced by meals, physical activity, efforts at concentration, things you read, and the weather. And your mood rises and falls like a ship on the waves. Ordinarily these variations are only minor; as long as you keep busy, you do not think about them; but as soon as you do have the time to think about them, and begin to think about them seriously, little explanations crowd into your mind, and you believe that they are causes, while they are really only effects. A perceptive man can always find a number of reasons for being sad if he is sad, and a number of reasons for being happy if he is happy. The same reason can often serve two different purposes. Pascal, who had physical ailments, was terror-stricken by the multiplicity of the stars; and the majestic shudder he experienced while looking at them resulted no doubt from the fact that he was getting chilled at his window without realizing it. Another poet, if he is in good health, will talk to the stars as if they were lady friends. And both men will say lovely things about the starry sky: lovely things that are entirely beside the point.

Spinoza said that man cannot avoid having passions, but that a wise man creates within himself such a range of happy thoughts that his passions, in contrast, become insignificant. Without trying to follow him in his difficult paths, we nevertheless can create for ourselves a large reserve of voluntary happiness composed of such things as music, painting, conversation, which will make our melancholy moods seem trivial by comparison. A man who frequents society forgets about his liver in the performance of his social obligations. We ought to

10 *

feel ashamed at not getting more out of a responsible and useful job, out of books, or friends. But perhaps it is a universal
error, and one of great consequence, to systematically refuse
to take an active interest in things of value. We count on them
to provide the interest. It can be a great art to will what we
are sure to desire.

22 February 1908

V

Melancholy

Not long ago I saw a friend who was suffering from a kidney stone and was quite despondent. Everyone knows how that kind of illness makes one feel depressed. I told him this, and he agreed; so I ended up by saying: "Since you know that this particular illness makes people depressed, you shouldn't be at all surprised that you feel depressed, and you shouldn't let it get you down." This bit of reasoning made him burst out laughing, which in itself was no small accomplishment. Still, and despite the rather ridiculous way I expressed it, it is perfectly true that what I said was important—something all too rarely taken into consideration by people who are afflicted with misfortunes.

Profound sadness is always the result of an unhealthy condition of the body. If an affliction is not an actual illness, before long it leaves us moments of peace, and many more than we realize. The thought of a misfortune astonishes rather than grieves us as long as fatigue, or some kind of stone lodged somewhere within us, does not begin to stir up our thoughts. Most men would deny this, and claim that what makes them suffer in their misfortune is that they keep thinking about how unfortunate they are. I admit that when we are unhappy, it is very difficult not to believe that some ideas have, as it were, claws and thorns, and that it is they that are torturing us.

Let us consider, however, those sick people who suffer from melancholy. We shall see that they can find reasons for being sad in any thought whatsoever. Every word you say wounds them. If you pity them, they feel humiliated and hopelessly miserable. If you do not pity them, they tell themselves that they have no friends and are completely alone in the world. Thus the churning of their thoughts only reminds them of the unpleasant condition to which their illness has consigned them; and while they are tearing themselves down, overwhelmed by the reasons they think they have for being sad, they are really savoring their sadness like true gourmets. So, in melancholiacs we can see an enlarged image of every distressed man. What is evident in them, namely, that their sadness is an illness, is surely true for all of us. The exasperation that comes from afflictions no doubt results from our repeated attempts to analyze them, which is like probing around a sore spot.

We can free ourselves from this kind of madness, which aggravates passions to the point of frenzy, by telling ourselves that sadness is only an illness and ought to be endured like an illness, without so many rationalizations and explanations. In this way, we put a stop to the endless succession of bitter words. We accept our affliction as if it were a stomach ache. We attain a state of mute melancholy, a kind of stupor almost without consciousness. We no longer accuse; we endure. However, we remain calm, and in so doing we combat sadness in precisely the right way. This is what prayer was aiming for, and it was not at all a bad solution. Before the immensity of its object, before the wisdom that knows all and has weighed all things, before the incomprehensible majesty and impenetrable justice, the pious man refrained from forming thoughts. There

* 13

is certainly no prayer, earnestly made, that has not had re-markable effects immediately. To vanquish frenzy is in itself an accomplishment. But simply by using common sense we can provide ourselves with the same kind of mental opium which deters us from counting up our misfortunes.

6 February 1911

On Passions

Passions are harder to bear than illnesses. The reason is, no doubt, that our passions seem to come entirely from our character and ideas, but at the same time have the appearance of absolute necessity. When a physical wound makes us suffer, we recognize in it a mark of that necessity which is everywhere around us; and all is well with us, except for the suffering. When confronted with an object which, because of its appearance, or the noise it makes, or its odor, causes a sudden fear or desire in us, we can still put the blame on things, and flee from them to regain our equilibrium. But in the case of passions, there is no hope; for, if I love or if I hate, the object of my passion need not be present before my eyes. I can imagine it, and even transform it by a subjective process much like poetry. Everything draws me back to it; my arguments are fallacious, and yet seem good to me; and often it is my intellectual lucidity which goads me on. One does not suffer so much from emotions. A good fright and you run, without giving a thought to what you are doing. But the shame of having been afraid, if you are made to feel ashamed, will turn into either anger or self-justification. Above all, your shame in your own eyes when you are alone, especially at night in a state of forced repose—that is when it is unbearable, for then you can savor it leisurely, so to speak, and without hope. All the shafts have been hurled by you alone, and they all fall back on you; you are your own worst enemy. When a man dominated by his passions convinces himself that he is not ill and that nothing is preventing him at that moment from enjoying life, he falls back on this reflection: "My passion is an integral part of me; and it is stronger than I am."

There is always an element of remorse and fright in passions, and with reason, it seems to me. For you can say to yourself: "Do I have to behave so badly? Do I always have to go over and over the same things?" Humiliation follows. And fear too, for you say to yourself: "It's my own thoughts that are poisoned; my arguments are directed against myself. What is this magic power that directs my thoughts?" Magic has found its proper place here. I believe that it is the force of passions together with internal slavery which have led men to think that occult powers and bad luck can come from a word or a glance. Since he is unable to call himself sick, the man dominated by his passions calls himself cursed; and this idea provides him with an endless amount of material to use for self-torture. Who could ever understand this violent suffering that is located nowhere? And the prospect of unending torment which only gets worse from one minute to the next makes these people rush to their death joyfully.

Many men have written on this subject. And the Stoics have given us some good arguments against fear and anger. But Descartes was the first, and he says so proudly, to get to the heart of the problem in his *Treatise on the Passions*. He demonstrated that despite the fact that passion is entirely a state of mind, it nevertheless depends on movements within our body. It is because of the movement of the blood and the course of that unknown fluid which travels through the nerves and brain that the same ideas come back to us, and so vividly, in the silence of the night. This activity within the body escapes us all; we see only its effects, or better still, we believe that it is the result of our passions when, on the contrary, it is movements in the body that nourish our passions. If we could fully comprehend this fact, we would save ourselves the trouble of having to analyze our dreams, or our passions, which are really dreams that are more cohesive. We would recognize the exterior necessity to which we are all subjected, instead of accusing ourselves and cursing ourselves. We would say: "I am sad; everything looks black to me; but external events are in no way responsible, and my thoughts are in no way responsible. It's my body that insists on reasoning. These are the opinions of my stomach."

9 May 1911

VII

The Demise of Oracles

I remember a certain gunner who used to read palms. He was a woodcutter by profession, and had learned from his solitary life how to interpret signs quickly. I suppose that by imitating some other fortuneteller he, too, began to take an interest in people's palms; and it was there that he read thoughts, just as others do by looking into another person's eyes or at the lines of his face. He had his temple in the forest known as the White Oaks and, by the light of a candle, was in all his majesty, telling people things about themselves that were often true and always reasonable, predicting the near future as well as the distant future of each one, which is no laughing matter. And it so happened that I had the opportunity of seeing one of his predictions come true, and no doubt I have embellished it a bit in my memory, for I took pleasure afterwards in rediscovering the prediction in the event. This trick of the imagination made me wary once again, and proved to me once more the wisdom of prudence, which I had always believed in; for I have never shown the lines of my palm to him or anyone else. The strength of incredulity lies in the refusal to consult oracles. As soon as you do consult one, you are forced to believe in it somewhat. Therefore, the demise of oracles, which marks the beginning of the Christian revolution, was no small event.

Thales, Bias, Democritus, and all the other famous old men of ancient times had, no doubt, abnormal blood pressure by the time their hair began to fall out; but they never suspected it, which was no small advantage. The hermits of ancient Thebaid were better off still; since they looked forward to death instead of fearing it, they lived a long life. If one were to make a very careful physiological study of worry and fear, one would see that they are illnesses which combine with other illnesses and aggravate them; thus the person who knows he is sick, having learned it beforehand from a medical oracle, is doubly sick. I can well understand how fear leads us to combat an illness by means of a regimen and medicines. But what regimen and what medicines will cure us of fear?

The giddiness which seizes us when we are on some high place is a real illness which is due to the fact that we mime the fall and the desperate motions of a falling man. This illness originates entirely in the imagination. So do the stomach cramps of someone about to take an examination; the fear of not being able to answer the questions is as effective as castor oil. With that in mind, consider the effects of continual fear. But in order to be prudent when dealing with prudence, it must be taken into consideration that the movements of fear tend quite naturally to aggravate the malady. He who is afraid of not being able to sleep is ill-disposed for sleeping, and he who is wary of his stomach is ill-disposed for digestion. Therefore one should imitate health rather than sickness. The details of this bit of gymnastics are not known to us, but you can wager that the gestures of politeness and good manners have something to do with health, in accordance with that theorem, of sorts, which states that the signs of health are none other than the movements that are consistent with healthiness. Bad doctors would, therefore, be those whom you like well enough to try to interest in your complaints. And good doctors would be those who, on the contrary, ask you in the usual manner: "How are you?", and then do not listen to your answer.

5 March 1922

VIII

On Imagination

When a doctor sews up a cut on your face—the result of some minor accident—among his instruments there is a glass of rum to revive a failing courage. Generally, however, it is not the patient who drinks the rum, but the friend who is watching and who, without really understanding what is happening to him, turns a sickly green and almost faints. Which goes to show that, contrary to what a famous moralist said, we are not always strong enough to bear the pains of others.

This example is worthy of consideration because it shows a type of pity that is not dependent on our personal ideas. The sight of those drops of blood and of that skin that resists the curved needle immediately provokes a kind of diffused horror, as if we were holding back our own blood, tightening our own skin. Thought is absolutely powerless in combating this effect of the imagination, because in this case imagination is completely independent of thought. The line of reasoning that wisdom might suggest would be obvious and very easy to understand, for it is not the spectator's skin that is being pricked. But this reasoning is completely ineffectual; rum is more persuasive.

And so I conclude that our fellowmen have great influence on us simply by their presence, simply by the indications of their emotions and passions. Pity, terror, anger, tears, do not wait for me to become intellectually involved in what I see. The sight of a horrible wound alters the face of a spectator, and this face in turn attests to something horrible and affects the diaphragm of the spectator's spectator even before he learns what the other person has seen. And a description, no matter how skillful, moves us less than that face which was moved by emotion. The stimulation of emotions is direct and immediate. Therefore it is very inaccurate to describe pity by saying that he who feels it is thinking about himself, and sees himself in the other man's place. This thought, when it does occur, comes only after one has felt pity. Through imitation, our body is soon predisposed to suffering, feeling at first a kind of vague anxiety. We demand of ourselves an explanation of this feeling that comes upon us like a sickness.

One could also give a rational explanation of dizziness. A man on the edge of a chasm might say to himself that he could fall in. But if he holds on to the railing, he will tell himself that now he cannot fall; dizziness rushes through him all the same, from head to foot. The first effects of our imagination are always in the body. I once heard the account of a dream in which the dreamer was present when an execution was about to take place, without knowing whether it was to be his own or that of someone else, and without his ever really thinking about it specifically. The only thing he did know was that he felt a pain in the vertebrae of his neck. Such is the effect of pure imagination. It seems to me that the dispassionate soul, who is always thought of as being noble and sensitive, is, on the contrary, simply indifferent. The living body is more admirable—the body, which our thoughts can make suffer and which action can cure. Not without a struggle; but real thought has something more to overcome than just a problem of logic; and it is the trace of a struggle that makes for beautiful thoughts. The metaphor in this heroic game is the role of the human body.

20 February 1923

Maladies of the Mind

Our imagination is worse than a Chinese executioner. It doles out fear; it makes us savor it like gourmets. A real catastrophe does not strike in the same spot twice; the blow crushes the victim; the moment before, he was just like us when we are not thinking about a catastrophe. A pedestrian is hit by an automobile, thrown sixty yards and killed outright. The drama is over; it hasn't really begun; it didn't last long; duration will come about through reflection.

Therefore, I who think about the accident judge it very inaccurately. I judge it from the perspective of a man who is always on the point of being hit, but never will be. I imagine the car approaching. In actual fact, I would jump aside if I saw it coming. But I do not jump aside because I put myself in the place of the man who was hit. I fashion for myself a kind of cinematographic view of my own destruction, but in slow motion; from time to time the camera stops completely. And I start over; I die a thousand times while very much alive. Pascal said that illness is unbearable for a person who is well precisely because he is well. We are no doubt sufficiently overcome by a serious illness so that we experience only what it does to us at any given moment. An actual fact has this much good, however bad it might be: it puts an end to the game of possibilities, it is no longer still to come, and it shows us a new future in a new light. A suffering man desires a state of undistinguished normalcy as if it were a marvelous happiness, a state which, the day before, would have perhaps made him unhappy. We are wiser than we realize.

A real ill moves quickly, like one of our executioners. He cuts off the hair and the shirt collar, ties the arms, gives his man a push. To me it seems long because I think about it, because I keep coming back to it, because I try to hear the sound of the scissors, to feel the hands of the assistants on my arm. In actual fact, each new impression drives out the last, and the real thoughts of the condemned man are probably something like the spasmodic twitches of a worm that has been cut in pieces. We insist on thinking that the worm is suffering; but in which of those pieces is the suffering of the worm located?

We suffer when we meet up with an old man who has become senile, or with a ruin of a drunkard who shows us "a friend's tomb." We suffer because we keep trying to see them as they are and, at the same time, as they were. But nature has gone her way; fortunately her changes are irreversible. Each new state made the following one possible; all this distress that you are amassing at any one point is dispersed along the road of time. It is the misfortune of the present that will bring forth the next moment. An old man is not a young man who suffers from old age; a man who dies is not a living man who enters into death.

That is why it is only the living who are grieved by death, only the happy who measure the weight of misfortune; and, to tell the truth, we can be more sensitive to other people's maladies than to our own, and without being hypocritical. The result is a false view of life which, if one does not watch out, will poison life. We must concentrate with all our strength and knowledge on the reality of the present instead of playing at tragedy.

12 December 1910

X

Argan *

It takes very little to spoil a beautiful day; for example, a shoe that pinches. Nothing can please you then, and your judgment is completely deadened. The remedy is simple; all this unhappiness can be shed as easily as a garment. We know it perfectly well; this kind of unhappiness is alleviated, even in the present, by knowledge of what causes it. An infant who feels the prick of a pin cries as hard as if he were desperately ill. This is because he has no idea of the cause or the remedy. And sometimes he even makes himself sick from crying, and then he only cries all the harder. That is what you might call an imaginary ill; for imaginary ills are as real as the other kind. They are only imaginary in that we sustain them through our own doing, all the while putting the blame on external things. Infants are not the only ones who cry themselves sick.

They say that ill humor is a sickness and that nothing can be done about it. That is why I'll begin by mentioning examples of suffering and annoyance that can be relieved by a very simple gesture. We all know that a cramp in the calf of the

* Translators' note: Argan is the principal character in Molière's comedy, *The Imaginary Invalid.*

leg will make even the strongest of men cry out; but stand up and put all your weight on that leg, and you are cured in an instant. If you rub your eye when you have a gnat in it, or a bit of dust, it will bother you for two or three hours; just keep your two hands still and look at the end of your nose; soon the flow of tears will relieve your discomfort. Since I first heard about this simple remedy, I have had occasion to use it more than twenty times. Which proves that it is best not to start immediately accusing people and things around us, but to look first of all to ourselves. We sometimes think we see in others a certain predilection for unhappiness; in certain types of insanity this tendency is very pronounced. We might easily imagine some sort of mystical or diabolical force at work. But we would be duped by our imagination; there is not that much profundity in a man who is scratching himself, and certainly no appetite for pain; there is just agitation and irritation, which are self-perpetuating until we understand what is causing them. Fear of falling from a horse comes from the awkward and frantic movements we make so as to prevent ourselves from falling. Worst of all, these movements scare the horse. From which I would conclude, like the Scythians, that when a man knows how to ride, he is master of himself—or almost. There is even an art of falling, amazing in the drunkard because he does not give a thought to falling properly, admirable in the fireman because he has learned from gymnastics how to fall without being afraid.

A smile seems to us a mere trifle which has no effect on our state of mind; and so we don't give it a try. But often politeness, forcing us to smile and extend a gracious greeting, changes everything for us. Physiologists are well aware of the reason; for the smile reaches down as deeply as the yawn and relaxes, one after the other, the throat, the lungs, and the heart. A doctor would not be able to find anything in his medicine bag that takes effect so quickly, so harmoniously. Here, imagination pulls us out of distress with a remedy no less real than the maladies it causes. Moreover, a person who wants to appear nonchalant shrugs his shoulders, which, if you think about it, aerates the lungs and calms the heart, in every sense of the word. For the word "heart" has several meanings, but you have only one heart.

11 September 1923

Medicine

"I know," says a scientist, "quite a number of truths, and I have a pretty good idea of those I don't actually know. I know what a machine is, and how everything can suddenly fall apart when a nut works loose, all for lack of a little care, for lack of a few minutes of attention, and always because an expert was not consulted at the proper moment. That's why I reserve part of my time for tending to this elaborate machine I call my body. That's why, as soon as there are any symptoms of grinding or grating, I turn myself over to an expert so that he can examine the part that is ill, or presumably ill. And by these preventive measures, according to the advice given by the illustrious Descartes, I am assured of prolonging my life, barring quirks of fate, for the full life expectancy of the instrument which I received from my ancestors. And there you have my bit of wisdom." Those were his words, but he lived a dreary life.

"I know," says an avid reader, "quite a number of false ideas that complicated men's lives back in the days of credulousness. These errors have taught me some important truths which our scientists are scarcely aware of. Imagination, according to what I have read, is king of the human world. And the great Descartes, in his *Treatise on the Passions,* has admirably explained to me the reasons why. For anxiety, even if I succeed in overcoming it, will inevitably upset my stomach. A surprise will inevitably change my heartbeat. And the mere idea of finding a worm in my salad makes me actually feel nauseated. All these absurd ideas, even if I don't believe them, take hold deep inside of me and grip my vital organs; suddenly, they modify the flow of my blood and body fluids, which my will power could never do. Whatever invisible enemies I might swallow with each mouthful of food, they cannot affect my heart or stomach any more drastically than the changes in my moods or the fantasies of my imagination. It is necessary, first of all, to be as contented as possible. In the second place, I must avoid constantly fussing over my body; there is no surer way of disturbing all the vital functions. For can we not find in the history of any people that there were men who died because they believed themselves cursed? Can we not find that hexes worked very well, as long as the interested party knew about them? And what can even the best doctor do except put a hex on me? What good can I expect from his pills when just one word from him is enough to change my heartbeat? I don't really know what I can hope for from medicine, but I know very well what there is to fear in it. And indeed, whatever malfunction I feel in this machine which I call me, my greatest consolation is in the thought that it is precisely my concern and my worry that cause almost all the disorder, and therefore that the best and surest remedy is to have no more fear of a stomach ache or a backache than I do of a corn on my toe. The fact that a bit of hardened skin can cause just as much suffering—now there is a good lesson in patience, don't you agree?"

23 March 1922

The Smile

Concerning ill humor, I should like to say that it is no less a cause than an effect. I am even inclined to believe that most of our illnesses result from a failure to be polite, which I see as a kind of affront that the human body directs against itself. My father who, because of his profession, spent a lot of time observing animals, used to say that, although subjected to the same conditions we are and just as prone to excesses, they have far fewer illnesses; this always surprised him. It is because animals do not have moods, that is to say, the irritation, fatigue, or boredom that are nurtured by our thoughts. For example, everyone knows that our mind is scandalized at not being able to sleep when it wishes, and, because of this concern, puts itself into a state in which sleep is impossible. At other times, fearing the worst, it provokes a state of anxiety with its unhealthy musing, which slows recovery. The mere sight of a flight of stairs, and our heart skips a beat—as we so appropriately say—through an effect of the imagination which cuts off our breath at the very moment we need to breathe deeply. And anger is really a kind of illness, exactly like a cough. One can even consider coughing a type of irritation, for indeed it has its origins in a condition of the body; but the imagination soon begins to expect the cough and even to desire it, foolishly believing it can get rid of the discomfort by exasperating it, like those people who keep scratching themselves. I realize that animals, too, scratch themselves, and even to the point of doing themselves injury; but it is the dangerous privilege of man to be able to scratch himself with his thoughts, if I may use that image, and, through his passions, to exert a direct influence on his heart, causing the blood to rush through his body.

Still, our passions can be managed. You cannot rid yourself of them just by wanting to; the only way it can be done is by a long, indirect method, like that of the man who is wise enough to refrain from seeking honors so that he will not be tempted to desire them. But ill humor binds, smothers and strangles us simply because we induce in ourselves a physical state which predisposes us to sadness, and in fact promotes sadness. A man who is bored has a way of sitting down, of getting up, of speaking, which is calculated to promote boredom. The irritated man has another way of tying himself up in knots; and a discouraged man unties, you could almost say unhitches, his muscles as much as possible instead of taking some action that would give him the vigorous stimulation he needs.

Acting against ill humor is not a question of using our judgment, which is totally ineffectual. We must change our stance and make the proper movements with our body, for the muscles that regulate our movements are the only part of us we can control. Smiling, shrugging the shoulders, are both familiar tactical maneuvers against worry. And notice how these movements, which are so easy to make, immediately modify the circulation of the blood. We can stretch at will and make ourselves yawn, which is the best form of gymnastics for anxiety and impatience. But it never occurs to an impatient man to feign indifference in this way; nor will the man who is suffering from insomnia ever think of pretending to be asleep. On the contrary, ill humor is very much aware of itself, and so perpetuates itself. Lacking mastery over ourselves, we have recourse to politeness; we seek situations where we will be forced to smile. That is why the company of people who are indifferent is so well liked.

20 April 1923

XIII

Accidents

Everyone has meditated for a moment or two on a terrifying fall. The enormous car lost a wheel and tipped over, perhaps rather slowly at first, and then the unfortunate passengers, suspended for a moment above the abyss, screamed inhumanly. Anyone can easily imagine the scene, and some people will dream about it, actually experiencing the fall itself, and bracing themselves for the impact. But then, they have enough time to mull it over; they reenact the whole thing; they savor the fear; they stop themselves from falling in order to think about what is happening. A lady said to me one day: "I'm afraid of everything, but still I'm going to have to die." Fortunately, the force of circumstances, once we are in its power, does not give us any leisure. It is as if the chain of time were broken; thus extreme suffering is nothing but the ghost of suffering—impalpable. Horror is soporific. Chloroform, it seems, deadens only the upper layers of thought; the multitude of organs continue their activities and suffering on their own; but that is not the end of it. All suffering strives to become an object of contemplation; otherwise it would not be felt at all. How serious can a pain be when it lasts only a fraction of a

* 35

second and is then forgotten? Suffering, such as a toothache, presupposes that we anticipate it, wait for it, and give it temporal duration by providing it with a past and a future; it is as if the present were nullified. We fear more than we actually suffer.

These remarks, which are the essence of any real consolation, are based on a careful analysis of consciousness itself. But imagination will make itself heard; it is especially good at concocting horror stories. Experience would indicate just how good. And indeed, we are not totally lacking in experience. Once, in a theatre, a brief moment of panic swept me some thirty yards from my seat. It was caused simply by the smell of something burning and by a rush toward the exits, which I instinctively imitated. What could be more horrible than being caught up in such a human torrent and swept along, you don't know where or why? I did not know what was happening, not then and not even afterwards when I thought about it. All I knew was that I had moved; and since I did not have time to deliberate, no thinking whatsoever was involved. There was neither expectation nor recollection. And so there was no perception or even feeling; only a sleep of a few seconds.

The evening I left for the war front, in that dreary train full of rumors, wild stories, and bizarre fantasies, I was beset with unpleasant thoughts. Among us there were a few men who had escaped alive from the Battle of Charleroi and who had had leisure enough to be afraid. To top it all off, in the corner there was a kind of corpse, very pale and with his head bandaged. The sight of him gave credence to the hideous descriptions of battle. "They came down on us," the narrator was saying, "in swarms; our guns couldn't stop them." Our imaginations were already in flight. Fortunately the corpse spoke up and told us how he had been killed in Alsace by a piece of shrapnel which struck him behind the ear—not an imaginary misfortune this time, but a real one. "We were running along under the cover of a forest," he said. "I came out into the open; but from then on I don't know that happened. It's as if the fresh air put me to sleep all of a sudden, and I woke up in the hospital, where they told me that they had taken out of my head a piece of shrapnel that was as big as my thumb." And so, by this other Er who had escaped from death, I was brought back from imaginary misfortunes to real ones; and I suspected that the greatest of all ills is wrong thinking. Which, however, did not completely cure me of imagining the brutal impact of the shrapnel and the crack of bones breaking in my head. But it is already something to know that misfortunes are never what we imagine them to be.

22 August 1923

XIV

Dramas

The survivors of that disastrous shipwreck have terrifying memories of it: the wall of ice seen through the porthole; the moment of hesitation and hope; then the picture of that huge, brightly lighted ship on the calm sea; then the prow which begins to sink; the lights that suddenly go out; all at once, the desperate cries of eighteen hundred people; the stern of the ship rising up like a tower, and all the machinery sliding forward with a deafening clap of thunder; finally, that huge coffin slipping gently under the waves; the cold night presiding over the solitude; after that, the bitter cold, the despair, and at last the rescue. A drama relived many times during those nights when they did not sleep; a drama whose scenes are now all pieced together, with each detail assuming tragic significance, just as in a well-written play.

When the sun comes up and shines on Macbeth's castle, a porter is there, watching the sunrise and the swallows—a picture of freshness, simplicity, and purity; but we know that the crime has been committed. Here tragic horror is at its apogee. Similarly, when that shipwreck is remembered, each moment is colored by what is going to happen next. Thus, the image of the

brightly lighted ship, tranquil and massive on the sea, was reassuring at the time; in the memories and dreams the survivors
will have of it, and in my image of it, this is a moment of horrible
anticipation. The drama unfolds now for a spectator who
knows, who understands, who savors the agony moment by moment; but when it actually occurred, that spectator did not
exist. There was no time to reflect; impressions changed along
with the spectacle; or more accurately, there was no spectacle
but only unexpected perceptions which were not interpreted
but which simply succeeded one another. Above all, there was
activity which submerged thought; at each instant, a thought
was shipwrecked; each image appeared and then died. The
event itself killed the drama. Those who died felt nothing.

To feel is to reflect, to remember. Everyone has had occasion
to note the same thing in both minor and serious accidents;
novelty, surprise, and urgent action take up all our attention, leaving no time for feelings. The man who tries in all
sincerity to reconstruct the actual event would have to say that
he was living in a kind of dream, without understanding what
was happening and without thinking about what could happen. But the terror which he now feels in thinking about it induces him to compose a dramatic story. That is the way it is
with great sorrows, as when you follow someone's illness until
he dies. At the time, you are almost stupefied, completely preoccupied with the events and impressions of each moment.
Even if you paint for others a picture of terror and despair,
you did not suffer at the moment it was actually happening.
And when people who have spent too much time thinking
about their troubles relate their woeful tale to others, they get
a bit of comfort out of telling it.

In any case, whatever the feelings of those who died might
have been, death has effaced everything. Before we even opened
our newspaper, their anguish had ended; they were cured—an

idea familiar to all of us; which makes me think that we do not really believe in a life after death. But, in the imagination of the survivors, the dead never stop dying.

24 April 1912

XV

On Death

The death of a statesman provides a good occasion for reflection; and amateur theologians suddenly appear everywhere. Each thinks about his own destiny and about our common fate; but his thought has no real object; we cannot conceive of ourselves as being anything but alive. Whence impatience. Faced with this abstract and completely amorphous menace, we do not know what to do. Descartes said that irresolution is the greatest of all evils. And so, there we are, plunged in irresolution, and with no possible solution. People who have decided to hang themselves are better off; they choose the spot and the rope; everything depends on them up to the last jump. And, just as the man who has gout is kept busy trying to find a comfortable position for his leg, so every condition, no matter how bad, demands some real attention and effort. But the case of a perfectly healthy man who thinks about death is almost absurd because the danger is so imprecise. This brief agitation, which is completely irrational and which can quickly get out of hand, is raw passion. A card game, for lack of anything better, will successfully provide an active thinker with well-defined problems, decisions to make, and specific issues to act upon.

Man is courageous; not just on occasion, but fundamentally. To act is to dare. To think is to dare. Peril is everywhere; but that fails to frighten man. You can see him seeking out death and defying it; but he cannot bear to wait for it. Men who are idle are bellicose because of their impatience. It is not that they want to die; it is rather that they want to live. And the real cause of war is certainly the boredom of a few men who yearn for clearly identifiable perils, neatly defined and even solicited, like those in a card game. And it is not just by chance that those who work with their hands are peaceable; it is also because they triumph continually. Their lives are full and positive. Repeatedly they vanquish death, and that is the only valid way of thinking about it. What preoccupies the soldier is not the abstract proposition of being subject to death, but a precise danger, and then another. It is entirely possible that war is the only cure for theological inquiry. Men who spar with shadows always end up by leading us off to war, for the only thing in the world that can cure us of fear is real danger.

Take even a sick man and see how quickly he is cured of his fear of being ill by the illness itself. It is always the imaginary thing that is our enemy because we cannot find anything to get a grip on. What can we do against suppositions? It happens that a man finds himself ruined; immediately he sees more than one thing he can do, and right then and there; thus he picks up the pieces and finds his life intact. But a man who lives in fear of being ruined and is miserable simply because he worries about revolutions, unpredictable changes, financial loss— what can such a man do? Whatever idea occurs to him is soon nullified by a contrary idea, for the range of possibilities is limitless. Thus, misfortunes are constantly reborn, and no progress whatsoever is made. All his actions are mere beginnings that block each other and become entangled. I believe that fear is nothing but ineffectual agitation, and that meditation always increases fear. Men fear death as soon as they start thinking about it; true; but what don't they fear as soon as they start thinking without acting? What don't they fear as soon as their thought gets lost in mere possibilities? One can get stomach cramps at the very thought of an examination. Judging by the way the intestines twist, might we not think that they are being threatened with a deadly weapon? Not at all. It is irresolution which, for lack of an object, sets the belly on fire.

20 August 1923

XVI

Postures

Even the most ordinary of men is a great artist when it comes to miming his own misfortunes. If his chest feels tight and oppressed, you will see him press his arms against it and tense all his muscles. In the absence of any enemy, he clenches his teeth, stiffens his muscles, and shakes his fist at the heavens. And even if these disturbing motions are not actually made, you may be sure that they are being acted out internally in the immobile body with even more powerful effects. When we cannot sleep, we are sometimes amazed that the same thoughts, nearly always unpleasant ones, keep going through our head. One could wager that what brings them back again and again is this acting out of our feelings. The cure for all moral ills, as well as for all other maladies in their incipient stages, is muscular relaxation and gymnastics. This remedy will, I believe, nearly always work; but no one ever thinks of it.

Polite behavior can strongly influence our thoughts. And miming graciousness, kindness, and happiness is of considerable help in combating ill humor and even stomach aches; the movements involved—gracious gestures and smiles—do this much good: they exclude the possibility of the contrary movements, which express rage, defiance, and sadness. That is why social activities, visits, formal occasions, and parties are so well liked. It is a chance to imitate happiness; and this kind of comedy certainly frees us from tragedy—no small accomplishment.

A doctor would do well to think about the position a religious man assumes in prayer; for the kneeling body, calm and supple, relaxes the internal organs and permits them to perform their vital functions with greater ease. "Bow your heads, proud Sigambri," said Drusus to this fierce Germanic tribe; they were not told to cure themselves of anger and pride, but first to be silent, to close their eyes, and to dispose themselves to gentleness. In this way, all the violence in their character was effaced; not for long, nor forever, because that is beyond our power, but for the time being. Religion's miracles are not really miracles.

It is a fine sight to see how a man drives a troublesome idea out of his mind. You will see him shrug his shoulders and breathe deeply, as if he were untangling his muscles. You will see him turn his head in order to turn his eyes and thoughts to other things. Then, with a bold movement, he will cast off his worries and snap his fingers, a gesture that often begins a dance. If, at that moment, David's harp should charm him, he might actually begin dancing, regulating and moderating his movements in order to smooth away all·anger and all impatience, and the melancholy man would soon be cured.

I like the gesture that indicates perplexity—a man scratching his head. For this ruse has the effect of diverting and disarming one of the most fearsome of gestures, that of preparing to throw a stone or a javelin. Thus the gesture of perplexity which releases one's feelings is very similar to the belligerent gesture which arouses them. The rosary is an admirable invention, for saying one's beads busies both the mind and the fingers. Better still is the wise man's secret, which is that man's will has no control over his passions, but does have direct control over his movements. It would be easier to pick up a violin and begin to play than to try to reason away our passions.

16 February 1922

XVII

Gymnastics

How can you explain that a pianist who is dying of fright as he walks on stage is immediately cured as soon as he begins to play? One might say that he no longer thinks about being afraid, and that is true. But I would rather examine more thoroughly the nature of fear itself, and thus realize that the pianist shakes off and unravels his fear by the supple movements of his fingers. For, since everything in our body is interrelated, the fingers cannot be relaxed unless the chest is also; suppleness, like stiffness, invades all parts of the body; and in a well-disciplined body, fear has no place. Singing and oratory also dispel fear by means of the measured movements which are required of all the muscles. It is worth noting, although too seldom noted, that it is not thought but action which frees us from passions. We cannot force ourselves to think as we wish. However, once accustomed to doing certain things, once the muscles are trained and exercised by gymnastics, we can act as we wish. In moments of anxiety, do not try to reason, for your reasoning will only turn against you. Instead, try those arm-raising exercises that are now taught in all schools; the results will astonish you. Thus the moralist sends you to a gymnast.

*

An aviator told me how he once spent two hours in mortal fear, lying on the grass, waiting for the clouds to break, and meditating on dangers he could do nothing about. As soon as he was in the air, performing the familiar task of handling his plane, he was cured. This story came back to me as I was reading about some of the adventures of the famous World War I aviator, René Fonck. One day he was flying a fighter plane at twelve thousand feet when he noticed that the controls were no longer functioning and that he was falling. He tried to find out what was wrong, and finally noticed that one of the shells had been knocked out of its case and was jamming the instruments. While still falling, he put the shell back in place and then managed without difficulty to turn his plane upwards. Such incidents, when remembered or dreamt, might frighten that courageous man even now. However, if one were to believe that he was as afraid when the incident took place as he might have been later when thinking about it, I believe one would be wrong. Our body is troublesome to us in this respect, that as soon as it no longer has any orders to follow, it acts on its own. But, on the other hand, it is so constituted that it cannot assume two different postures at the same time; a hand must either be open or closed. If you open your hand, you release all the irritating thoughts that you were holding in your closed fist. A simple shrug of the shoulders, and the worries that were locked up in your chest are forced to flee. It is the same thing as not being able to swallow and cough at the same time, which is how I explain the effectiveness of lozenges. Similarly, you would cure yourself of hiccups if you could manage a yawn. But how does one go about yawning? One succeeds very well by first miming, by executing a series of simulated stretches and yawns. The same body which is hiccuping without your permission will thus be forced into a yawning position, and will indeed yawn. A powerful remedy against hiccups, coughs, and against worries. But show me the doctor who will order his patients to yawn every fifteen minutes.

16 March 1922

XVIII

Prayers

You cannot hear in your imagination what a closed *e* sounds like by opening your mouth wide. Try it, and you will notice that your *e*, unpronounced and existing only in your mind, will become a kind of *ah*. This example shows that the imagination cannot go very far if the motor organs of the body execute movements that thwart it. Gestures are direct proof of this relationship, since they betray all the impulses of the mind. If I am angry, I clench my fists instinctively. This is well known, but we do not generally use this knowledge to formulate a method for regulating our passions.

Every religion contains prodigious practical wisdom. For example, to counteract the rebellion of a man who has suffered a misfortune but who refuses to face up to the fact, who wears himself out and redoubles his misfortune by useless agitation, it is better to force him to kneel down with his head in his hands than to try to reason with him. For, by this bit of gymnastics, and that is the word, you thwart the violent state of his imagination, and for a moment you halt the effects of despair and anger.

But as soon as men are swept along by their passions, they

are astonishingly naive. They simply cannot believe in such simple remedies. A man who has been offended will first think of a thousand things that confirm the offense; he will look for circumstances that aggravate it, and will find them; precedents, and will find them. "These," he will say, "are the causes of my justifiable anger. I certainly do not intend to put down my weapons and forget about it." Such is the first reaction. Then the faculty of reasoning will enter the picture, for men are amazing philosophers; and what amazes them most is that reasoning has no effect on their passions. "My better judgment tells me every day. . . ." We all say this kind of thing; and something would be missing from the tragedy if the soliloquizing hero did not exhaust every argument that pleads in his favor. This situation, clarified by the Skeptics, is what gives credence to the idea of invincible fate; for the Skeptic invented nothing. The earliest idea of God, as well as the most sophisticated concepts have always originated in man's feeling that he is being judged and condemned. During the long infancy of humanity, men believed that their passions as well as their dreams came from the gods. And every time they felt alleviated, as if they had been freed from these burdens, they attributed it to a miracle of grace. A man who is extremely irritated kneels down to ask for comfort, and naturally obtains it if he really does kneel down—in other words, if he assumes a posture that is incompatible with anger. He later tells how he felt the presence of a beneficent power that delivered him from evil. And note how theology develops naturally. If he obtains nothing, some counselor or other will easily point out to him that it was because he did not ask properly, because he did not really kneel down, and finally, because he was too attached to his anger, which truly proves, so the theologian will say, that the gods are just and that they see into our hearts. And the priest was just as naive as the believer. Men suffered from their passions for a long time before suspecting that movements of the human body were what caused them, and thus that suitable gymnastics were the remedy. And having noticed the powerful effects of posture, of ritual, and let us say, of politeness, men for a long time regarded as miracles those sudden changes of mood which are called conversions. And superstition, it appears, always consists in explaining real effects by supernatural causes. And still today even the most learned find it hard to believe, when in the throes of passion, what they know perfectly well.

24 December 1913

XIX

The Art of Yawning

A dog yawning by the fire is a sign to hunters that they should put off their worries until the next day. This manifestation of life, stretching itself boldly and unceremoniously, is delightful to see and impossible to resist. Everybody around begins stretching and yawning, which is the prelude to sleep. Not that yawning is a sign of fatigue; this thorough aeration of the internal organs is, however, a repudiation of attentiveness and argumentativeness. Nature announces by this energetic reform that she is content with just being alive, and tired of thinking.

Anyone can observe that concentration and surprise inhibit breathing. Physiology completely erases all doubts about it by showing how the powerful muscles used in self-defense act on the thorax and inevitably contract and paralyze it as soon as they come into play. And it is remarkable that raising the arms above the head, the sign of capitulation, is also the surest way to relax the thorax; but it is also the ideal position for yawning energetically. With that in mind, we should be able to see how any sort of worry literally oppresses the heart, soon spreads to the thorax, and causes anxiety, which is the sister of anticipation; for we are anxious only when we are in a state of expectation, even if the thing anticipated has little importance. This painful state is soon followed by impatience, which is anger that is directed against oneself and that brings no relief. Social rituals engender all these discomforts, which are further aggravated by formal dress and by contagion, for boredom is infectious. But yawning is the contagious remedy for those contagious rituals. One wonders how yawning can spread like a disease. I think, rather, that seriousness, circumspection, and a worried attitude are what spread like a disease. But yawning, which is a reassertion of life and, as it were, a return to health, spreads by the rejection of seriousness, and is like an emphatic declaration of insouciance; it is the signal that everyone has been waiting for, like the signal to break ranks. This sense of well-being is irresistible; all the seriousness was leading up to it.

Laughter and tears are solutions of the same order, but more limited, less sure; a struggle takes place between two contradictory thoughts, one of which leads to enslavement, the other to liberation. Whereas the yawn sweeps away all thoughts, those that enslave as well as those that liberate; contentment effaces them all. Thus it is always the dog who yawns. Everyone has probably noticed that yawning is always a hopeful sign in what are called nervous disorders, where thought causes the illness. But I believe that yawning, just like the sleep that follows, is beneficial in all illnesses. And it is an indication that thoughts always play a large part in our illnesses—not a very astonishing observation when you think about how painful it can be to bite your tongue; the figurative sense of this expression suggests that regrets for having spoken, so aptly called pangs of conscience, can cause even physical pain. Yawning, on the other hand, involves no risks.

24 April 1923

XX

Ill Humor

According to the laws of exasperation, nothing is better than scratching yourself. It is a way of choosing your pain, of taking revenge on yourself. A child tries this method first. He cries, and his crying makes him cry all the harder; he gets upset because he is angry and consoles himself by refusing to be consoled, which is what sulking is. Hurt those you love and then hurt them some more in order to punish yourself. Punish them in order to punish yourself. Ashamed of being ignorant, vow to read nothing more. Be obstinate about being obstinate. Cough in indignation. Search the memory for any insult; make it even more pointed; with the skill of a tragedian, repeat to yourself whatever wounds and humiliates you. Interpret things according to the principle that the worst is the truest. Imagine yourself surrounded by nasty people so that you will then be obligated to be nasty. Attempt things without hope of success and say after failing: "I would have bet on it; that's just my luck." Everywhere show a bored face and find others boring. Do your best to be unpleasant and then be surprised when others do not find you pleasant. Try frantically to fall asleep. Cast doubt on every joy. Show a sad face at everything and object to everything. Create worse moods out of bad moods. While in this state, judge yourself. Tell yourself: "I'm shy; I'm gauche; I'm losing my memory; I'm getting old." Make yourself out to be ugly and then look at yourself in the mirror. Such are the traps of ill humor.

That is why I do not scorn people who say: "It's bitterly cold out; there's nothing better for the health." For how could they do better than that? Rubbing your hands is doubly good when the wind blows from the northeast. Here, instinct is as good as wisdom, and the reaction of the body is like a reaction of joy. There is only one way to resist cold, and that is to be happy about it. And, as that master of contentment, Spinoza, would say: "It is not because I am getting warm that I am happy; rather it is because I am happy that I am getting warm." In the same way, then, we should always tell ourselves: "It is not because I have succeeded that I am happy; rather it is because I was happy that I succeeded." And if you go out looking for joy, be sure you take along with you a good supply of joy. Be thankful before receiving anything. For hope gives rise to reasons for hoping, and a good omen makes the event happen. Let everything, therefore, be a good omen and a favorable sign; "A black cat augurs happiness if you want it to," said Epictetus. And by that he did not only mean that we should find happiness in everything, but more particularly, that genuine hope turns everything into a source of happiness because it changes the course of events. When you meet up with a bored man, who is also a boring man, you should first of all smile. And if you want sleep to come, have confidence that it will come. In short, no man can find in this world a more formidable enemy than himself. I described above the life of a kind of lunatic. But lunatics are nothing but examples of our errors magnified. In the slightest touch of ill humor there is a miniature persecution mania. And certainly I do not deny that this kind of madness is caused by some imperceptible lesion some-where in the nervous system which determines our reactions; every irritation ends up by entrenching itself. It is just that, in considering these madmen, I look for something that can be useful to us; that "something" is a dangerous miscalculation which they show us enlarged, as if under a magnifying glass. These poor souls ask the question and give the answer; each acts out all the parts in his play. Magical incantations; effects always follow. But understand why.

31 December 1921

XXI

On Character

Everybody has moods depending on the wind and on his stomach. One man kicks the door, another smites the air with words that have no more meaning than the kicks. The great in spirit let these incidents slip into oblivion; whether others are responsible for them or they themselves, they pardon completely, for they never think about them. But it is common to venerate one's ill humor and, as it were, to vow to be ill-humored; this is how we make our own character; and because one day you were rather peevish with someone, you come to like him less. To pardon oneself in such a case is rarer than it should be; and often it is the prerequisite for pardoning others. On the other hand, a kind of extreme remorse is often what magnifies the other person's error. Thus each of us parades his cultivated ill humor, saying: "That's the way I am." This always says more than we realize.

It sometimes happens that we cannot bear certain fragrances. This ill humor directed against bouquets and colognes is not constant. But seeking out and sniffing the faintest fragrance, and swearing that it will give you a headache, is indeed common. We swear to anything—for example, that smoke makes us cough. Everyone has known family tyrants. The man who suffers from insomnia swears that he will not be able to sleep. And if he has decreed that the slightest noise wakes him up, there he is, lying in wait for every little noise, ready to accuse the whole household. He may go so far as to become irritated with himself for having slept, as if he had failed to be sufficiently vigilant in maintaining his character. Anything can become an infatuation, even losing at cards, which I have seen.

There are people who begin to fear that they are losing their memory, or that they can no longer really express themselves. Proof is not long in coming, and this comedy, which is quite sincere, sometimes turns into tragedy. One cannot deny real illnesses or the effects of old age; but doctors long ago noticed the dangerous tendency to systematize which compels the patient to look for symptoms that he finds only too easily. This process of amplification is almost totally responsible for our passions and for a considerable number of our illnesses, especially mental illnesses. Charcot, the distinguished neuropathologist, finally arrived at the point of refusing to believe anything his patients said about themselves; and one can affirm that certain illnesses have disappeared, or almost, because of the incredulity of doctors.

Freud's ingenious system, famous for a time, is already losing its influence because it is simply too easy to implant any idea one wishes in the mind of a worried man who, as Stendhal said, already has his imagination for an enemy. Without taking into account the fact that sex, on which Freud's system is based, is precisely one of the things that becomes important through the significance we attach to it and through a kind of untamed poetry, as we know only too well. A doctor's thoughts are never good for the patient; everyone knows that. What is not so well known is that the patient promptly guesses what the doctor is thinking and makes that thought his own, which confirms the most brilliant hypotheses. In this way, amazing illnesses of the memory have been described—illnesses in which memories of a certain kind would all be lost, systematically. It had been forgotten that the tendency to systematize is present in the patient too.

4 December 1923

XXII

Fate

We do not know how to begin anything, not even when it comes to stretching out our arm; nobody begins by giving an order to his nerves or his muscles; the movement begins by itself; our business is to follow it along and to complete it as best we can. Thus, never deciding, we are always in a position of directing, like a coachman who reins in a horse. But he can only rein in a horse that has bolted; and that is what is called starting off; the horse is startled and runs; the coachman directs this spurt of energy. Similarly, a ship, if it has no forward thrust, cannot obey the helm. In short, the important thing is to get started no matter how; then there will be time to ask yourself where you are going.

Just who has made a choice? I ask you. Nobody has made a choice, since we all start out as children. No one has made a choice but everyone has acted before choosing; thus our careers are the result of natural forces and of circumstances. That is why people who deliberate never decide; and there is nothing more ridiculous than those schoolroom analyses of motives and causes; so it is that an abstract tale, which smacks of a grammarian's way of thinking, shows us Hercules choosing between vice and virtue. Nobody chooses; we are all moving along, and all roads are good. The art of living consists first of all, it seems to me, in not bickering with oneself over the road one has taken or the kind of work one does; but instead, in doing it well. We want to see the hand of fate in those choices we find already made and which we have not made; but such choices are not binding on us, for there is no lot that is inherently bad; every lot is good if one wishes to make it so. There is no more indubitable sign of weakness than debating about the qualities nature has endowed us with; nobody has a choice in the matter; but whatever these natural qualities are, they are enough to satisfy the most ambitious man. To make a virtue of necessity is our great and admirable task.

"Alas, why did I not study?" That is a lazy man's excuse. Study then! I do not believe that having studied is such a marvelous thing if one has given up studying. To count on the past is just as foolish as complaining about the past. Nothing that you have done is so good that you can rest on your laurels, nor so bad that something cannot be salvaged from it. I am even inclined to believe that good luck is more difficult to take advantage of than bad luck. If you were born with a silver spoon in your mouth, beware. What I find admirable in a man like Michelangelo is the fiery will that takes charge of the natural gifts and makes of an easy life a difficult one. This man, who was without a trace of complacency, had a head of white hair when, as he put it, he went to school to try to learn something. That shows irresolute people that any time is a good time to exert your will. And wouldn't a sailor laugh at you if you told him that the whole crossing depends on the first turn of the helm? However, that is what we try to make children believe; fortunately they scarcely listen; but still too much, if they go so far as to formulate the metaphysical concept that induces them to play out their whole existence on $a + b = ab$. This baneful concept does not influence them much in childhood, and harms them only later, for it is the excuse of weakness that makes men weak. Fate is a Medusa's head.

12 December 1922

XXIII

The Prophetic Soul

An obscure philosopher used the term "prophetic soul" to define a certain state of attentive passivity, if one may call it that, in which our thoughts yield to every force that comes along, like the leaves of a poplar. It is the soul on the alert, vulnerable, a kind of target. A state of fright. I understand the Sibyl, her tripod, her convulsions. Attentive to everything means fearful of everything. I pity those who do not know how to obliterate all the noise and movement of this great universe.

Sometimes an artist would like to fall back into the state of being receptive to everything, to all colors, all sounds, all warmth, all cold. He is then astonished that a peasant or a seaman, so deeply engrossed in the natural world and so dependent on it by his very situation, does not notice all these nuances. There is a splendid movement of the shoulders which unburdens us of all these things; it is a royal gesture. Saint Christopher crossed the water without counting the waves. "You don't sleep," he said, "when you're too clever"; you wouldn't be able to act either.

We must clear away, simplify, eradicate. The thing that characterizes man, it seems to me, is that he relegates every kind of half-sleep to sleep itself. It is a sign of good health when one cannot indulge in reveries for long, but drops off to sleep right away. And waking up is a rejection of sleep; but the prophetic soul half awakens and keeps on dreaming its dreams.

We can live like that; there is nothing to stop us. We are all so made that we can have some foresight into the future. If we take into account how the living body is constructed, we will realize that we register even the smallest external signs and record them within us. A certain sound of the wind heralds from afar the approaching storm; and certainly it is good to be attentive to such signs; however, we should not be alarmed at the slightest changes. I once saw a large barometer, so sensitive that a cart moving in the vicinity or even just a man's footsteps would make the needle jump. That is the way we would be if we just let ourselves go; our moods would change with the movements of the sun.

When a timid man finds himself with a group of people, he wants to hear everything, take in everything, interpret everything. And to him the conversation is as stupid and incoherent as if everyone were saying just whatever popped into his mind. But the wise man prunes the signs and the talk, like a good gardener. This is even more important out in the world; for everything would affect us and impede us; the horizon would block our view like a wall. But we consign things to their proper places; all thought is a massacre of impressions.

A weeding out. I knew a sensitive lady who suffered when she saw a tree or branch being cut. But without the woodcutter, we would soon witness the return of brushwood, snakes, swamps, fevers, hunger. Similarly, we must all clear away our moodiness. To deny our own moods is the essence of incredulity. This world is opened with a billhook and an axe; they carve out paths at the expense of illusions; they are a kind of defiance hurled at predictions. However, as soon as we become indulgent toward ourselves and begin to worship impressions, the world closes in on us; it makes its presence known. Cassandra prophesies misfortunes. Beware of Cassandras, somnolent souls. A real man bestirs himself and makes the future.

25 August 1913

XXIV

Our Future

Until we have grasped the fact of the interdependency of all things and the relationship between cause and effect, we will be overwhelmed by the future. A dream or a word from a fortuneteller will kill all our hopes; there are omens at every turn of the road. A theological concept. Everyone knows the legend of the poet who was warned that a house would fall down on him and kill him; he stayed out in the open. But the gods were not to be outdone, and an eagle dropped a tortoise on the poet's bald head, mistaking it for a stone. There is also the story of a king's son who, according to an oracle, was to be killed by a lion. They kept the boy at home with the women; but one day he became enraged at the sight of a tapestry that depicted a lion, scratched his fist on a rusty nail in his fury, and died of gangrene.

The idea that emerges from these stories is that of predestination, which theologians later made into a doctrine; and it goes like this: the destiny of each one of us is inalterable no matter what we do. Which is not in the least scientific, for this kind of fatalism amounts to saying: "Regardless of what the causes are, the effect will be the same." But we know that if the cause is different, the effect will be different. And we can destroy the specter of an inevitable future with the following reasoning: suppose I know that I'll be crushed to death by a particular wall, on a particular day, at a particular hour; this knowledge will in itself prevent the prediction from coming true. And that is the way we live; we dodge a misfortune at every moment because we anticipate it; thus what we anticipate, and this certainly makes sense, does not happen. An approaching automobile would run over me if I stayed in the middle of the street; but I don't stay there.

Just where does this belief in destiny come from? From two main sources. First of all, fear often thrusts us into a misfortune that we expect to happen. If somebody has predicted that I shall be run over by an automobile, and if this thought crosses my mind at a critical moment, it is enough to prevent me from acting as I should. For the thought that is helpful to me at such a moment is that I am going to escape unharmed, and I act to escape immediately. On the other hand, the thought that I am going to stay there paralyzes me through just the same mechanism. A kind of giddiness has made the fortune of fortune-tellers.

It might be added that each of our passions and vices is well endowed with the strength to arrive at its goal by any road it might take to get there. We can predict that a gambler will gamble, a miser will hoard, an ambitious man will scheme. Even without a fortuneteller we cast a kind of spell on ourselves by saying: "That's the way I am; I can't do anything about it." That, too, is a kind of giddiness, and one which also makes predictions come true. If we really understood the continual changes taking place around us, the variety and continual flowering of little causes, it would be enough to keep us from concocting a destiny for ourselves. Read *Gil Blas*; it is a lighthearted book, and it teaches us that we cannot count on having either good or bad luck, but that we must lighten the ship and let ourselves be carried by the winds. Our errors perish before we do. Let us not mummify them and keep them around.

28 August 1911

XXV

Predictions

I know someone who showed his palm to a fortuneteller in order to know his future. He told me he did it just for fun, and didn't really believe in it. Even so, I would have advised him against it, if he had asked me, because it is a dangerous way to have fun. It is very easy not to believe, as long as nothing has yet been said; for then there is nothing for you or anyone else to believe. Disbelief is easy at the outset, but soon becomes difficult; fortunetellers know this very well. "If you don't believe in it," they say, "what are you afraid of?" And thus the trap is set. As for me, I am afraid of believing, for who knows what they will tell me.

I suppose there are fortunetellers who believe in themselves. Those who only mean to joke might predict ordinary and likely events in ambiguous terms: "You will have troubles and a few little failures, but you will succeed in the end"; "You have enemies, but they will eventually come around to your point of view, and meanwhile, the constancy of your friends will console you"; "You will soon receive a letter concerning your present problems." . . . This list could be extended almost indefinitely, and such predictions are perfectly harmless.

However, if a fortuneteller thinks of himself as a real fortuneteller, then he might very well predict dreadful misfortunes for you; and you, levelheaded person that you are, you
would laugh. It is no less true, however, that his words would
stick in your memory and come back unexpectedly in your
musings and dreams, troubling you just a bit, until the day
when events seem to bear them out.

A girl I knew had her palm read one day by a fortuneteller
who told her: "You will get married; you will have a child; you
will lose it." Such a prediction is not too heavy a burden to
carry in the early stages. But time passed. The girl got married,
and just recently had a child; the prediction now weighs more
heavily on her mind. If the child should get sick, the fatal
words will resound deafeningly in the ears of the mother. Perhaps she had laughed at the fortuneteller. He will be avenged.

All sorts of things happen in this world, fortuitous occur-
rences that can shatter the most steadfast belief. You laugh
when something sinister and unlikely is predicted; you will
laugh less if part of this prediction comes true; then, even the
most courageous man will wait for the rest to occur. We all
know that our fears cause us as much suffering as the catastrophes themselves. It is possible for two prophets who do not
know each other to predict the same thing. If this concordance
does not upset you more than your intelligence tells you it
should, then I admire you.

As far as I am concerned, I prefer not to think about the future, but to look ahead only to what lies directly before me.
Not only will I not go showing the inside of my hand to a
fortuneteller, but more importantly, I will not try to read the
future by attempting to penetrate the nature of things; for I
do not believe that our sight extends very far, no matter how
great our knowledge. I have noticed that anything important
that happens to anyone is unforeseen and unforeseeable. Once

you have cured yourself of curiosity, you will no doubt then have to cure yourself of prudence.

14 April 1908

XXVI

Hercules

Man's only resource is his own will; an idea as old as religions, marvels, and misfortunes; but an idea which, by its very nature, is vanquished at the same time as the will itself; for inner strength is proved through its accomplishments. Hercules proved himself in this way until the day he saw himself become a slave; he then preferred a glorious death to a miserable life. This myth is the most beautiful of them all. If I had my way, children would be told about Hercules' labors so that they would learn to overcome external forces; for that is what living is all about, and the other choice—the cowardly choice —is nothing but a slow death.

I like a boy who reflects while overcoming difficulties and who, when he has taken a wrong road, says right away, "It's my fault," tries to find out where he made his mistake, and gives himself a friendly tongue-lashing. But what can you do with an automaton in the form of a man who always looks for excuses in the things and people around him? There is no joy along that road, for it is only too clear that the things and people around us pay little attention to an unhappy man; and so his thoughts shift with the wind, like the leaves in this harsh season. I find it remarkable that those who look for excuses outside of themselves are never happy, while those who immediately acknowledge their own mistakes and say, "I was really stupid," become strong and happy through the experience they have assimilated.

There are two kinds of experiences, one which weighs down and the other which lightens. Just as there is a happy hunter and a sad hunter. The sad hunter misses his rabbit and says: "That's just my luck" and adds, "Things like that happen only to me." The happy hunter admires the rabbit's cunning, for he knows that it is not in the rabbit's nature to pop into the stewpot. Proverbs are full of virile wisdom, and there is considerable profundity in what my grandmother used to say about larks—that they don't fall down at your feet already roasted. As we make our bed, so we must lie. "If only I could learn to like music," says the foolish man; but we must make the music; otherwise there is no music.

Everything is against us; but it is more accurate to say that everything is indifferent and disinterested; without the efforts of man, the face of the earth would be brushwood and pestilence; not hostile, but not friendly. There is nothing favorable to man except what he has made through his own efforts. But it is hope that makes for fear; that is why an accidental success is a very bad way to begin; and he who thanks the gods will soon curse them. Like those newlyweds who have affection for the official who issued the wedding license and for the church doorman; they did not see the sacristan's expression when he snuffed out the candles. One day I noticed the smile of a lady who had a perfume boutique; she turned it off the minute she closed her door. And it is also quite a sight to watch a shopkeeper put up his shutters; as soon as something unfamiliar—and this also includes a person—reveals to us the individual law by which it operates, then we can set about performing the

workers. How would they get up to the top branches? It would take tree surgeons. I know of only two in this area."

"Two," I told him, "that's already something. They'll take care of the top branches. Others, who are less experienced, will use ladders. And even if you don't save all your trees, at least you'll save two or three."

"I don't have enough energy for all that," he finally said. "I know what I'll do. I'll go away for a while so as not to see the invasion of the beetles."

"Oh the power of the imagination," I answered. "Here you are already routed before you've even begun to fight. Don't look beyond the task at hand. We would never do anything if we considered the immense weight of things and the weakness of man. That is why we must act, and think in terms of action. Look at that mason; he turns the crank calmly; the huge stone just barely moves. However, the house will get finished, and children will play on the stairs. I once felt admiration for a worker who was getting ready to bore a hole, with his brace and bit, in a wall of steel that was six inches thick. He whistled while turning the handle; fine flakes of steel fell like snow. I marveled at the man's courage. That was ten years ago. You may be sure that he got that hole drilled, and many others too. The beetles themselves can teach you a lesson. What's a beetle compared to an elm? But all those tiny nibbling mouths can devour a forest. We must have faith in our little efforts and use the tactics of an insect to fight against an insect. There are hundreds of things in your favor; otherwise there wouldn't be any elms. Destiny is not constant; a snap of the fingers, and a new world is created. The smallest effort produces incalulable results. The person who planted these elms did not reflect on the brevity of life. Like him, throw yourself into action and don't look beyond tomorrow, and you will save your elms."

5 May 1909

XXVIII

To the Ambitious

Everyone has what he wants. Youth is mistaken on this point because the only thing it really knows how to do is wish and wait for manna. However, no manna falls from the sky; and all the things we desire are like a mountain that waits and that we cannot avoid seeing. But we must climb it. I have observed that all ambitious people who get off to a good start arrive at their destination, and even faster than I would have believed possible. It is true that they never failed to take whatever steps were expedient, never failed to frequent those individuals they expected to make use of, nor to avoid those useless individuals who are nothing more than pleasant. In short, they flattered when it was necessary. I cast no blame; it is a question of taste. The point is that if you take it upon yourself to tell unpleasant truths to a man who is in a position to open doors for you, do not say that you wanted to pass through them; you dreamed that you were passing through them, as we sometimes dream that we are a bird. It is as if you dreamed of being a diplomat without having the bother of formal meetings and without having to think about being circumspect. I have known a goodly number of lazy people who say: "They'll come to me.

I'll not lift a finger." The truth of the matter is that deep down they want to be left alone, and they are. Thus they are not so unhappy as they would like to believe. Fools are people who make a mad rush toward their goal, snatching at a rich prey in one fell swoop, like a hawk. Nothing can be expected from these poorly planned expeditions. In a like manner, I have seen men of ability attack a safe with their fingernails. From which it is sometimes concluded that society is very unjust, which is an unjust conclusion. Society gives nothing to the man who asks for nothing, I mean, firmly and persistently; and that is not a bad thing, for education and aptitude are not the only things that count. Some men might know a good deal about politics but, by the fact that they do not engage in it themselves, they let it be known that they do not like the seamy side of the trade, and all trades have their seamy side. And what does it matter then if they are knowledgeable and have good judgment since they do not like the trade? Barrès received visitors, made recommendations, remembered much. I do not know if he was well suited for the affairs of state; but he certainly did like the trade.

As I said before, all who want to get rich manage to do so. That scandalizes people who have dreamed of having money, and who do not have any. They looked at the mountain; but it just waited for them. Money, like every other advantage, demands fidelity above all else. Many people imagine that they want to make money simply because they must. But money eludes those who pursue it simply out of need. People who have made their fortune have done so by striving to dominate something. But the man who would like a nice little business where he could be happy in a nice friendly atmosphere, where he could indulge his preferences and fancies, where he could be easygoing and even generous—such a man evaporates like rain on a hot pavement. It takes rigor, and it takes courage;

in sum, one must prove oneself in hardship, like the knights of old. Mercury does not combine with gold more quickly than profits accrue to him who totals up his accounts every day and every hour. But the frivolous lover is judged and condemned. He who insists on spending will earn nothing. And that is the way it should be, for what he wants is to spend, not earn. I knew an amateur farmer who planted for his own pleasure, and in a way for his health. All he wanted was to break even; but such equilibrium is never found. He ruined himself quite thoroughly. There is a kind of avarice peculiar to old people, and even beggars, which is a mania; but the avarice of a merchant is part of the trade itself. If what one wants is to make money, one must also will the necessary means, that is, tally up every little profit. Otherwise it is like climbing without paying attention to each step one takes; not every stone is firm, and gravity never loosens its hold on us. Ruin is a good word; for loss clings to the merchant and keeps tugging at him. He who does not feel this other kind of gravity is wasting his time.

21 September 1924

XXIX

On Destiny

"Destiny," said Voltaire, "leads us along and laughs in our face." This statement surprises me, coming from Voltaire who, to a great extent, determined the course of his own life. External destiny acts through violent means; it is clear that a stone or a bullet will kill a Descartes with equal effectiveness. These forces can efface any of us from the face of the earth in a moment. But the event which so easily kills a man is not able to change him. I marvel how people approach their final hour, and how they turn everything to account; like a dog who transforms the chicken he is eating into the flesh of a dog and the fat of a dog, so the individual assimilates events. Constant exercise of the will, which distinguishes men of strong character, always ends up by making its mark in the world of changing things where anything is possible. The characteristic of a strong man is that he stamps everything with his seal. But this strength is more common than one might believe. Everything is a garment for man, and the folds conform to his body and his movements. A table, a desk, a room, a house are promptly arranged or thrown into disorder depending on the hand that touches them. Events occur, important or unimportant; and we say that they are favorable or unfavorable based on an out-side judgment; but the man who manages them well or badly always makes his hole according to his own shape, like the rat. Take a good look; he has done what he wanted to do.

"Whatever we desire when we are young we have in abundance when we are old." Goethe cites this proverb at the beginning of his memoirs. And Goethe is a brilliant example of those men who fashion every event according to their own formula. It is true that not everyone is a Goethe; but everyone is himself. The imprint he leaves may not be particularly admirable; but he does leave it everywhere. What he wants may not be anything terribly exalted; but what he wants, he has. Moreover, this man who is not Goethe did not want to be. Spinoza, who better than anyone understood men of a croco-dilian and invincible nature, said that man does not need the perfection of a horse. Similarly, no man would know how to make use of Goethe's perfection. But the merchant, no matter where he is, even in the midst of ruins, buys and sells, the banker makes loans, the poet sings, the indolent sleep. Many people complain about not having this or that; but the reason is always that they did not really want it. The colonel who retires on a farm in the country would have liked to have become a general; but if I could examine his life, I would find some little thing that he neglected to do, that he did not want to do. I could prove to him that he did not want to become a general.

I see people who, although they have sufficient means, have not made much of a mark for themselves. But what did they want? To be frank? They were. To avoid flattering? They did not flatter and still don't. To judge, counsel, refuse? They do. That man has no money? But was he not always scornful of money? Money goes to those who honor it. Show me just one man who wanted to get rich and who did not manage to do so. I mean, who willed to. To hope is not to will. The poet hopes for ten thousand francs; he doesn't know from whom or how; he doesn't make the slightest movement toward those ten thousand francs; and so he doesn't have them. But he is a creator of beautiful poetry. Therefore, that is what he does. Beautiful, in accordance with his nature, just as the crocodile fashions its hide and the birds its feathers. This internal force which ends up by making its mark may also be called destiny; but the only thing that this kind of life, so well fortified and organized, has in common with the roof tile that accidentally killed Pyrrhus, is that they are both called destiny. Which is what a wise man explained to me when he said that Calvin's predestination was not so very different from liberty itself.

30 October 1923

X X X

The Power of Forgetting

The correctional method which consists in curing a drunkard by having him swear an oath bears the stamp of action; a theoretician would have no confidence in it, for in his eyes habits and vices are clearly defined and well established. Following the method of the physical sciences, he insists that every man has within him various ways of reacting that are similar to properties, like those of iron or sulfur. But I believe it more likely that very often virtues and vices are not in our nature, any more than it is in the nature of iron to be hammered or laminated, or of sulfur to be in gunpowder or in cannons.

In the case of a drunkard, I can easily see the cause; here it is habit that creates the need; for drinking what he drinks makes him thirsty and deprives him of his reason. But the basic motives for his drinking are very weak; an oath can squelch them; and beginning with this mental effort, our man soon becomes as sober as if he had drunk nothing but water for the past twenty years. The opposite can also happen; I am not much of a drinker; but I could soon become a drunkard, and with no effort at all. I used to like to gamble; circumstances having changed, I haven't thought about it any more; if I took it up again, I know I would like it. There is a stubbornness in our passions and perhaps most of all an enormous error; we believe that we are hooked. People who don't like cheese do not want to try any of it because they think that they won't like it. Often a bachelor believes that he would find marriage unbearable. Despair, unfortunately, brings with it a certitude, or let us say a strong conviction, that makes us reject any sort of alleviation. This delusion, for I believe it is one, is quite natural; we cannot judge accurately what we do not have. While I am drinking, I cannot conceive of sobriety; I reject it by my very acts. As soon as I no longer drink, I thereby reject drunkenness by that act alone. The same is true for sadness, for gambling, for everything.

As the time for moving approaches, you say goodbye to the walls you are going to leave; no sooner is your furniture in the street than you already like your new house; the old house is forgotten. Everything is soon forgotten. The present has its strength and its youthfulness, always; and we accommodate ourselves to it with confidence. Everyone has experienced this, and yet no one believes it. Habit is a kind of idol that has power because we obey it; and here it is our thought that deceives us; for what we cannot imagine seems impossible for us to do. Imagination, because it cannot free itself from habit, controls man's world; and it should be noted that imagination cannot invent anything; it is action that invents.

My grandfather, when he was about seventy, took a dislike to solid foods, and lived on milk for at least five years. They said it was a mania; they were right. One day at the family dinner table I saw him suddenly attack a chicken leg; and he lived another six or seven years, eating like you and me. An act of courage, to be sure, but what was he defying? The opinion of others, or his opinion of the opinion of others, or rather his opinion of himself. An unusual man, some might say. Not at all. We are all like that, but we don't realize it; and we all continue playing our role.

24 August 1912

XXXI

In the Great Meadow

Plato tells fairy tales, pretty much like all fairy tales, but which, because of certain little words tossed off as if in passing, reverberate in the depths of our being and suddenly light up unfamiliar recesses. Such is the story of a certain Er who had been thought dead after a battle, then returned from Hades once the error was discovered, and related what he had seen down there.

The most dangerous ordeal that had to be gone through was the following: the souls, or shades, or whatever you want to call them, are led out into a great meadow, and sacks containing a destiny for them to choose are thrown down in front of them. The souls still remember their past life; they choose according to their desires and regrets. Those who wanted money above all else choose a destiny full of money. Those who had a lot of it want to have still more. Sensualists look for sacks full of pleasures; the ambitious look for a royal destiny. In short, each finds what suits him, and, shouldering their new destinies, all go off to drink the waters of the river Lethe, which means the river of Forgetfulness, then head once again for the world of men, to live as they have chosen.

A singular ordeal and a strange punishment, much more dangerous than it seems. For few men reflect on the true causes of happiness and unhappiness. Those few go back to the source, that is to say, back to the tyrannical desires that put a check on reason. They mistrust riches, for wealth makes us sensitive to flattery and deaf to those who are unhappy. They mistrust power, for it renders all who have it more or less unjust. They mistrust pleasure, for it obscures and finally extinguishes the light of intelligence. Those sensible men are therefore going to scrutinize carefully more than one attractive-looking sack, always mindful of maintaining their equilibrium and not risking, in a brilliant destiny, the bit of clear judgment they have managed to acquire and preserve with so much difficulty. They will carry off on their backs some obscure destiny that no one else would want.

But the others, who spent their lives galloping after their desires, feasting on whatever seemed good to them without looking any further than the platter—what can you expect them to choose except more blindness, more ignorance, more lies and more injustice? And so they mete out their own punishment, more severely than any judge would. A millionaire may now be in the great meadow. And what is he going to choose? But let's stop using metaphors; Plato is always much closer to us than we realize. I have had no personal experience concerning a new life which is said to come after death; to say that I do not believe in it is therefore an understatement; I have no way of even conceiving of it. I would say, rather, that the life to come, where we are punished according to our own choice and even according to our own law, is precisely the future into which we are constantly slipping and where each of us unwraps the package he has chosen. And it is also true that we never stop drinking from the river of Forgetfulness, accusing the gods and fate. He who has chosen ambition did not realize that he was choosing base flattery, envy, injustice; but they came in the package.

5 *June 1909*

XXXII

Attitudes toward Neighbors

"How unpleasant it is," someone says, "to live with people we know too well. We unreservedly bemoan our fate and thus increase our little miseries; and they do likewise. We are quick to complain about their activities, their remarks, their opinions; we give vent to our passions; we have fits of anger over trivial things; we are too sure of attention, of affection, and of forgiveness; we have revealed ourselves too thoroughly to try showing only our good side. This constant candor does not give a true picture; it exaggerates everything, accounting for the acerbity of tone and the petulance of behavior which is astonishing in the most closely knit families. Politeness and formality are more useful than we realize."

"How unpleasant it is," someone else says, "to live with people we don't know at all. There are miners underground who are chipping away for a stockholder. There are seamstresses wearing themselves out for the coquettish customers of a department store. At this very moment there are poor souls assembling and gluing together, at very low pay, toys by the hundreds for the pleasure of rich children. Neither the rich children, nor the elegant ladies, nor the stockholders give a thought to these things; but they all pity a lost dog or a lame horse; they are polite and good to their servants, and cannot bear to see them red-eyed or with hurt feelings. People give big tips, and not hypocritically, for they see the joy of the waiter, of the deliveryman, of the cabdriver. The same man who pays a porter handsomely for carrying his trunks will affirm that railroad workers can live comfortably on what the company gives them. Everybody continually tries to get away with as much as he can; and society is a marvelous machine which allows decent people to be cruel without realizing it."

"How pleasant it is," a third person says, "to live with people we don't know too well. Everyone keeps a tight rein on his words and gestures, and consequently on his anger. Good humor shows on people's faces and soon is in their hearts. We don't even think of saying the kind of thing we would later regret. We show our best side to people who don't know us very well; and this effort often makes us fairer toward others, and toward ourselves. We expect nothing from a man we don't know; we are very happy with whatever he does give us. I have noticed that foreigners are quite pleasant because the only things they can say are polite expressions, without barbs; that's why some people enjoy being in a foreign country; they have no opportunity to be unpleasant, and are more satisfied with themselves while they are there. Even apart from the conversations, what friendliness, and what easy companionship you find out on the sidewalk! There, an old man, a child, even a dog can move about freely; in the street, on the other hand, drivers hurl insults at each other; everyone is pushed along by travelers who don't even see each ·other; the machine is not complicated, but already it is grating. Social stability will come about only through direct relationships, broad social consciousness, direct exchanges; not through organizations such as unions and governmental bodies, which are machines, but through a sense of community in each neighborhood which should be neither too big nor too small. Federalism by region is the best kind."

27 December 1910

XXXIII

Family Life

There are two types of people: those who become accustomed to noise, and those who try to silence others. I have known many people who fly into a rage if a voice murmurs a few words or if a chair is moved a bit noisily while they are working or trying to sleep. I have known others, however, who scrupulously avoid telling those around them what to do; they would rather lose their train of thought or a couple of hours of sleep than interrupt their neighbors' talking, laughing, and singing.

These two types of people shun each other and associate only with those of their own type. This explains why the rules and regulations of family life vary so much from one family to another.

There are families in which it is tacitly agreed that whatever offends one member will be avoided by all the others. One member of the family is bothered by the smell of flowers; another by loud talking; one insists on quiet in the evening, while another cannot bear noise in the morning. One of them refuses to permit religious discussions; another clenches his teeth as soon as the conversation turns to politics. Each is granted the power of veto, and they all exercise it majestically. One of them will say: "I'll have a headache all day because of those flowers." Another one adds: "I didn't sleep a wink last night because of that door that somebody slammed around eleven o'clock." The dinner hour is like a session of Parliament with everyone airing grievances. Each member knows all the complicated rules, and children are brought up with the precise goal of being taught to obey them. Finally, everyone just sits around staring at each other, talking about only the most inoffensive trivialities. This results in a dreary kind of peace and a stultifying happiness. The only thing is, since each person ends up feeling that there are more demands made on him than he makes on the others, each considers himself a noble soul and repeats with conviction: "One must not live for oneself alone; one must think of others."

There are also other families where the whim of each member is sacred and cherished, and where it never occurs to anyone that his pleasure might disturb the others. But let us not talk about those people; they are egoists.

12 July 1907

XXXIV

Solicitude

We all know the famous scene in *The Barber of Seville* in which Basile, who is told by everyone, "You look terribly pale," ends up believing that he really is sick. I think of this scene every time I find myself with a closely knit family, where each member watches over the health of the others. Woe to him who is a little pale or a little flushed; the whole family questions him with a note of anxiety in their voices: "Did you sleep well?", "What did you eat yesterday?", "You're working too hard," and other such comforting words. Then come the stories of illnesses "that were not treated in time."

I pity the sensitive and slightly cowardly man who is loved, coddled, pampered, and looked after in that way. The little miseries of everyday life, such as indigestion, coughs, sneezes, yawns, muscular pains, will soon become dreadful symptoms for him; and he will follow their progress with the help of his family and under the indifferent eye of a doctor who, as you can well imagine, is not going to keep on reassuring such people at the risk of looking like a jackass.

As soon as we are worried about something, we lose sleep. And so our imaginary invalid spends his nights listening to his heartbeat and his days telling about his nights. Soon, his illness is understood and known by everyone; it gives new life to dying conversations; this unfortunate man's health has a market value, like stocks and bonds; at times it is on the rise, at times it falls; and he knows it or guesses it. There is now one more neurasthenic in the world.

The remedy? Get away from one's family. Go live among people who are indifferent, and who will ask you distractedly, "How are you?", but will flee if you answer seriously, people who will not listen to your complaints and will not watch over you with that tender solicitude which used to tie your stomach up in knots. Under these conditions, if you are not immediately driven to despair, you will get well. Moral: never tell anyone that he looks sick.

30 May 1907

Domestic Tranquility

I am thinking once again about Jules Renard's frightening novel, *Poil de Carotte*. This book is pitiless, and it is worth noting with regard to it that it is always easy to see the bad side of things; generally it is passions which come out in the open and friendship which remains hidden. And the greater the intimacy, the truer this is. A man who does not realize this is necessarily unhappy.

In a family, and especially if all the members are completely devoted to each other, no one stands on ceremony, no one wears a mask. Thus a mother, in the presence of her child, will never think of trying to prove to him that she is a good mother; if she does, it is because the child is mean to the point of ferocity. A good child must therefore expect to be treated inconsiderately now and then; that is his just reward. Politeness is for people toward whom we feel indifferent, and moods, both good and bad, are for those we love.

One of the consequences of mutual love is that ill humor is indulged in ingenuously. The wise man will consider this a proof of confidence and spontaneousness. Novelists have often noted that the first sign of a woman's infidelity is a return to politeness and attentiveness toward her husband. But it is wrong to see this as a calculated move; it is simply that the spontaneousness is no longer there. "And what if I like to be beaten . . ."; this theatrical expression exaggerates to the point of ridiculousness a truth about the human heart. To beat, insult, accuse—that is always the first impulse. By this excess of confidence, a family can destroy itself, by which I mean become an odious group where voices automatically assume the accent of the most virulent anger. And that is easy to understand; in such close contact, day in and day out, the anger of one person nourishes that of another, and the most insignificant passions increase and multiply. It is thus very easy to describe all such sour moods; and if only people understood them, they would see that the remedy comes along with the ill.

People naively say about someone they know well who is cross and cantankerous: "That's just his character." But I do not believe too much in the idea of character. For, judging by experience, what is regularly repressed loses its importance to the point of becoming negligible. In the presence of his king, a courtier does not dissimulate his ill humor, he abolishes it by his intense desire to please; one movement excludes another; if you extend your hand amiably, that excludes a punch with your fist. It is the same for feelings, which derive all their intensity from gestures that are begun and then checked. A lady who is entertaining and who is annoyed by an unexpected guest interrupts her annoyance to welcome him; that does not prompt me to say: "What hypocrisy!" but: "What a perfect remedy for annoyance!"

Family structure is like judicial structure; it does not just happen; it is made and preserved by will power. He who has really understood all the danger implicit in the first impulse controls his gestures, and thus preserves the feelings that are important to him. That is why marriage must be considered indissoluble in terms of the will. Because then one makes every effort to preserve it by calming the storms. That is why vows are useful.

14 October 1913

XXXVI

On Private Life

It was La Bruyère, I believe, who said that there are good marriages, but no delightful ones. Humanity will have to extricate itself from these bogs created by false moralists, according to whom we taste happiness and then pass judgment on it as if it were a piece of fruit. But I maintain that even for a piece of fruit we can do something to help it taste good. This is even truer for marriage and every other human relationship; these things are not meant to be tasted or passively accepted; they must be made. A relationship is not like a bit of shade where one is comfortable or uncomfortable depending on the weather and the way the wind is blowing. On the contrary, it is a place of miracles, where the magician makes the rain and the good weather.

Each of us does a great deal to advance his business or his career. But generally we do nothing to advance our happiness at home. I have already written quite a lot on politeness, certainly without praising it as much as it deserves. And I am not saying for a moment that politeness is a lie, good for the foreigner; I am saying that the more sincere and precious our feelings are, the more they have need of politeness. A mer-

chant who would say "Go to the devil" would believe that he
was expressing his thoughts; but that is the trap of the passions. In our lives, everything that presents itself directly to our
senses is false. I open my eyes on awakening, and everything
I see is false; my task is to judge, to evaluate, and to put
things back in their proper perspective. The first sight of anything is a dream that lasts an instant, and dreams, no doubt,
are but brief stirrings of the mind without judgments. So, how
can you expect me to do any better at judging my immediate
feelings?

Hegel said that the immediate soul, or the natural soul, is
always enveloped in melancholy and somehow overwhelmed.
That impressed me as being remarkably profound. Reflections
about ourselves that fail to do us any good are a dangerous
game. And he who questions himself always gives unsatisfactory answers. Thought which does nothing but contemplate itself is boredom, or sadness, or worry, or impatience. Try it.
Ask yourself: "What shall I read to help pass the time?" You
are already yawning. You must get started. Desire fades if it is
not caught up by the will. And these remarks are enough to permit us to judge psychologists, who would have each of us me-
ticulously study his own thoughts, just as plants or shellfish are
studied. But to think is to will.

What is done so well in public—commerce and industry—
where everyone controls himself and continually corrects himself, does not succeed so well in private life. Everyone just lets
himself fall back and rest on his affections. Good for sleeping;
but in the half-sleep that characterizes the family, everything
can easily turn sour. That is why the finest people are often
driven to appalling hypocrisy. Something worth noting: we use
a kind of will power to hide our feelings, instead of using our
will to change them by setting ourselves in motion, like a gymnast. The belief that ill humor, sadness, and boredom are facts

like rain and wind is in reality a first impression, and it is false. And, in short, true politeness consists in feeling what one ought to feel. We constrain ourselves to be respectful, discreet, to be just. The latter is worth thinking about; a sudden return to justness, after the initial impulse of the passions, is certainly not typical of a robber; rather, it is characteristic of those who have developed probity, and without hypocrisy. Why should this not also be true for love? Love is not natural; and desire itself does not last long. But true feelings are of our own making. We do not play cards simply to fling them away at our first impulse of impatience or boredom; and no one has ever seriously thought of sitting down at a piano and striking the keys at random. Music, of all possible examples, is the best; for it cannot be sustained, even in singing, except through will power; grace comes later, as theologians have sometimes said without really knowing what they were talking about.

10 September 1913

XXXVII

The Couple

Romain Rolland, in his fine book, suggests that it is rare to find a happily married couple, and that this is natural. Pursuing the same line of thought and considering the characters in his novels, but especially people I have encountered, I can see distinctive traits that often make the two sexes hostile toward each other without their really knowing why. One of the sexes is affective, the other active; this has often been said and rarely explained.

Affective is not the same as affectionate. What is implied in the word is a closer bond between thought and the sources of life; this bond may be observed in all people when they are ill, regardless of their sex; but it is normally more pronounced in women, because of the natural predominance of the functions of pregnancy and nursing, and all related activities. This results in changes of mood whose causes are natural, but whose effects often give the appearance of fantasy, incoherence, and obstinacy. Without the slightest hypocrisy; for it takes profound insight, which is very rare, to explain the true causes of a mood, considering that the true causes also change our motives. If an almost imperceptible sense of fatigue saps my desire to take a walk, it will also provide me with reasons for staying at home. In our use of the word modesty, we often imply a dissimulation of true causes; I believe that it is rather an ignorance of true causes and a kind of natural, almost inevitable, transposition of things related to the body into language appropriate to the soul. A man in love finds this incomprehensible.

The other sex cannot be understood outside the context of action. Its proper function is to pursue, to build, to invent, to strive. Outside of these paths, it gets bored, but always without realizing it. The result is perpetual agitation over trivial things; by concealing it, his good will aggravates the agitation. He needs a diet of politics or industry. And it is common for women also to interpret as hypocrisy something that is a natural consequence. We can see crises of this kind profoundly analyzed in Balzac's *Memoirs of Two Young Married Women,* and especially in Tolstoy's *Anna Karenina.*

The remedy for these ills seems to me to be found in relationships with other people, and it works in two ways. First, the relationships with friends and relatives help establish in one's own home the same kind of politeness, absolutely necessary in order to dissimulate all the caprices of feeling which have only too many opportunities to express themselves. Dissimulate, that is the right word; the first stirrings of a mood are not even felt when one has no way of exhibiting them; that is why, however much one may be in love, politeness is more sincere than ill humor. And then too, social relationships occupy a man's mind and turn him from the idleness of complacency, in which he never feels comfortable, however much he tries. That is why there is always something to fear for a couple that lives on love alone, cut off from the rest of the world. Such households are boats that are too fragile, too unstable in the water, lacking ballast. And wisdom that comes from reflecting on the subject will have little effect. It is the institution that safeguards the feelings.

14 December 1912

XXXVIII

Boredom

When a man no longer has anything to build or to destroy, he is very unhappy. Women, I mean those who spend their days dawdling around the house and cooing at babies, will no doubt never understand why men go to cafés and play cards. To live with oneself and meditate about oneself is useless.

In Goethe's admirable *Wilhelm Meister,* there is a "Renunciation Society" whose members have agreed never to think about the past or the future. This rule, to the extent that one is able to follow it, is a very good one. But to be able to follow it, our hands and eyes must be occupied with something. Perception and action are the true remedies. If, instead, you twiddle your thumbs, you will soon sink into fear and regret. Thinking is a kind of game that is not always very healthy. That is why the great Rousseau wrote: "The man who meditates is a depraved animal."

Necessity extricates us, nearly always. Most of us have a job, and that is all to the good. What we lack are little jobs to provide relaxation from the main one. I have often envied women because they knit and embroider. Their eyes have something real to follow; as a result, images of the past and of the future seem vivid only in occasional flashes. But in those gatherings where a lot of time is wasted, men have nothing to do and buzz like flies in a bottle.

Those hours of insomnia, when we are not ill, are so feared, I believe, only because the imagination is then too free and has no real objects to contemplate. A man goes to bed at ten o'clock, and until midnight he flops around like a fish out of water, invoking the god of sleep. The same man, at the same hour, if he were at the theatre, would completely forget his own existence.

These reflections help us to understand the various occupations that fill the lives of the rich. Rich people provide themselves with endless duties and endless tasks, and run after them as if they were running to a fire. They make ten visits a day and rush from the concert hall to the theatre. The more energetic ones throw themselves into hunting, war, or perilous journeys. Others drive fast cars, and impatiently wait for the chance to break their bones in an airplane. They need new activities and new perceptions. They want to live in the world and not within themselves. Just as giant mastodons devoured forests, so they devour the world with their eyes. More ordinary people play at getting punched in the nose and stomach; that brings them back to things of the present, and they are then very happy. Wars are perhaps first of all a remedy for boredom; that would explain why people who are most likely to accept war, if not actually to desire it, are often those who have the most to lose. Fear of dying is the thought of an idle man, and is soon effaced by an urgent situation that demands action, however dangerous it may be. A battle is no doubt one of the circumstances in which we think least about death. Thus this paradox: the more we live a full life, the less afraid we are of losing it.

29 January 1909

XXXIX

Speed

I have seen one of the new locomotives, longer still, higher, more streamlined than the others; its mechanism is as carefully finished as that of a pocket watch; it rolls along almost noiselessly; one senses that all its movements have a precise function and that everything contributes to the common goal; the steam does not escape without having used up all the energy it received from the fire to make the pistons move; I can well imagine its smooth start, uniform speed, steady pressure without jolts, and the heavy convoy sliding along at more than a mile a minute. Moreover, the huge tender tells a lot about the amount of coal that is burned.

Here we have an example of something that took a great deal of knowledge, planning, testing, and a great deal of work with hammer and file. And why? To gain perhaps a quarter of an hour on the time it takes to go from Paris to Le Havre. And what will they, the happy travelers, do with this quarter of an hour so dearly bought? Many will spend it on the platform waiting; others will stay a quarter of an hour longer in a café, reading the newspaper even down to the classified ads. What has been gained? And for whom?

Speed

A curious phenomenon: the traveler, who would be annoyed if the train went less rapidly, will spend a quarter of an hour before his departure or after his arrival explaining that this train takes a quarter of an hour less than others to make the trip. Every man wastes at least a quarter of an hour a day chatting about things of similar worth, or playing cards, or daydreaming. Why could he not just as well waste that time sitting in a train?

Nowhere is one better off than in a train; I mean specifically express trains. One is very comfortably seated, better than in any armchair. Through large windows one sees rivers, valleys, hills, towns, and cities pass by; the eye follows roads along the hillside, cars on the roads, and lines of boats on the rivers. All the riches of the country are spread out before you: now wheat and rye, now fields of sugar beets and a refinery; then splendid timberlands, and after that, pastures, cattle, and horses. Excavations expose the earth's strata. Now there is a marvelous geography book that you can leaf through easily, and that changes every day, with the seasons and the weather. You may see a storm gathering behind the hills and hay wagons hurrying along the roads; another day, harvesters are working in gilded dust, and the air vibrates in the sun. What sight can compare with that?

But the traveler reads his newspaper, tries to be interested in the bad engravings that adorn the train compartment, pulls out his watch, yawns, opens his suitcase, closes it. The minute he arrives, he hails a cab, and runs off as if his house were on fire. In the evening, you will find him at the theatre. He will admire the painted cardboard trees, the fake harvests, a fake belfry. Fake harvesters will bellow in his ears; and he will say, rubbing his knees that have been bruised by the box in which he is imprisoned: "The harvesters are singing off key; but the scenery is not bad."

2 July 1908

XL

Gambling

"I pity a man who lives alone," someone said, "who has no needs or worries that he cannot take care of himself; I pity him as soon as he begins to feel the effects of old age or illness; for then he will think too much about himself. A family man, who is always worried about something and who cannot manage to free himself from debt, is much happier, despite appearances, because he does not have time to think about his digestion." There you have a reason for holding on to a few little debts, or for consoling yourself if you do have some.

When people are advised to lead an average kind of life, tranquil and secure, it is not made sufficiently clear to them that they will need a great deal of wisdom to be able to bear it. All things considered, contempt for riches and honors is easy; what is very difficult is to keep from getting too bored once you do find them contemptible. The ambitious man is always running after something, believing that he will find a rare happiness in it; but his principal happiness is in being kept busy; and even when he is unhappy because of some disappointment, he is still happy in his unhappiness. For he can see a remedy; and the true remedy is in seeing a remedy. The necessity which is spread out like a great country, perfectly visible, and outside ourselves, is always better than the necessity which is coiled up and which we feel deep within us.

Passion for gambling exposes this need for adventure in all its nakedness, as it were, without any extraneous ornamentation; for the gambler is never in a secure position, and I believe that it is precisely this which attracts him. Therefore, the true gambler is not very interested in games in which concentration, prudence, or skill considerably reduce the element of chance. On the contrary, a game like roulette, in which he does nothing but wait and take chances, fascinates him all the more. In a sense, his catastrophes are deliberate; for he tells himself at every moment: "The next turn of the wheel can ruin me, if I let it." It is like a very dangerous voyage of exploration, but with the difference that, by a simple change of thought, he could find himself back in the safety of his own home. This explains the attraction of games of chance; for nothing compels one to participate, and one takes risks only if one so wishes. This power is enjoyable.

War, no doubt, has an element of gambling; it is boredom that makes for war. And the proof is that it is always the man who has the least work and fewest worries who is the most bellicose. If you thoroughly understand these causes, you will be less moved by resonant proclamations. The rich, idle man seems admirable when he says: "Life is easy for me; if I expose myself to so many perils, if I gladly run these terrible risks, it can only be that I am doing so because I see some invincible reason or some inevitable necessity." Hardly. He is only a man who is bored. And he would be less bored if he worked from morning to night. Thus the unequal distribution of wealth has this disadvantage on top of everything else: it condemns to boredom a large number of men who are well fed. As a result, they manage to provide themselves with fears and angers that keep them busy. These deluxe emotions are poor people's heaviest burden.

1 November 1913

XLI

Hope

A fire made me think of Insurance, a goddess who, like Fortune, is by no means loved. She is feared; she is given meager offerings, without enthusiasm. And it is easy to understand why; the benefits of insurance become evident only at the time of a misfortune. The best thing is not having a fire; but not having a fire is normal, like having arms and legs, and we do not think about it. Considering that this happiness is negative, the money we pay for it seems foolishly wasted. Only big companies pay the premiums unconcernedly, just as they pay for everything else; but I often pity the captains of industry who do not know at the end of a day whether they have made a profit or taken a loss; no doubt their real pleasure comes principally from the power they exert over an army of underlings.

People who have big hopes and small means do not like insurance. Can you imagine a tradesman who would insure against total loss? Nothing would be easier if tradesmen pooled the profits that exceeded their normal returns. Thus the affiliated firms would, on the whole, prosper, and fairly well; the member tradesmen would be like civil servants, assured of a fixed income and retirement benefits; assured, if they so wished, of a doctor, a surgeon, a convalescent home; assured of a honeymoon trip and of a succession of pleasure trips. It is the essence of wisdom; and it is very attractive, theoretically. But it must be kept in mind that as soon as our material life is thus assured, or insured, in the fullest sense of the word, all our happiness still remains to be fashioned. Boredom lies in wait for him who has no resources within himself, and soon gets hold of him.

The goddess Lottery, whom the ancients called blind Fortune, is much more tenderly worshipped. Here, immense hopes, and on the other side of the coin, the mere fear of not winning, which is nothing. If one can imagine an office of every possible kind of insurance, these words should be written above the door: "Leave all hope behind, you who enter here." Which would place all the merchants of hope in a very favorable position. This is not merely because of our ambition, which is basically vanity, but rather because of the indefatigable inventiveness which always precedes action, and gives light and joy to every trade. Perrette, in the fable, does not see repose in her milk jug, but rather work. Calf, cow, pig, chickens, all require care. Each of us, in his daily tasks, discovers other tasks that he would like to plunge into. Hope knocks down the wall and perceives rows of vegetables or rows of flowers in place of overgrown weeds and brushwood. Assurance and insurance imprison.

Passion for gambling is an excellent example to consider. Man comes to grips with pure chance, which he has deliberately sought after and created. There is a free insurance plan against gambling losses; it consists in not playing. But almost all those who have some spare time eagerly play cards or dice, worshipping the inseparable twin sisters, hope and fear. And it may be that man is prouder of winning through good luck than he is of playing well. Which is expressed in the word congratulate; for to congratulate is precisely to praise success and not merit. The favor of the gods, an ancient idea that has survived the gods. If man were not like this, egalitarian justice would have prevailed long ago, for it is not difficult to achieve. But man does not really like things that are not difficult. Caesar reigns through the ambition of all of us; he represents the crowning of our hope.

3 October 1921

XLII

Taking Action

All racers willingly accept many hardships. All soccer players willingly accept many hardships. All boxers willingly accept many hardships. Sometimes we read that men seek pleasure; but that is not at all apparent; it seems, rather, that they seek hardships and that they like hardships. Old Diogenes used to say: "Hardship is the best thing there is." One might say in this connection that they all find pleasure in the hardships they are seeking; but that is playing with words; we should say happiness, and not pleasure; and they are two very different things, as different as slavery and liberty.

We want to act, we do not want to be acted upon. All those men who willingly accept so many hardships dislike, no doubt, forced labor; no one likes forced labor; no one likes the misfortunes that happen; no one likes to be compelled by the inevitable. But as soon as I willingly accept hardships, I am immediately happy. I am writing these reflections apropos of this and that. An author who makes his living by writing might say: "That certainly is a lot of hard work"; only no one forces me to do it; and this work which I have willingly chosen is a pleasure, or more accurately, a form of happiness. The boxer does not like the knocks that come his way; but he does like those he goes out to get. There is nothing so pleasant as a difficult victory, as long as the combat depends on us. Fundamentally, the only thing we like is power. By the monsters that he sought out and destroyed, Hercules proved his power in his own eyes. But as soon as he fell in love, he realized that he was enslaved and understood the power of pleasure; all men are like that; and that is why pleasure makes them sad.

A miser deprives himself of many pleasures, and fashions for himself an intense happiness, first by triumphing over pleasure, and then by amassing power; but he wants to be indebted only to himself for it. He who becomes rich by inheriting wealth is a sad miser, if he is a miser; for all happiness is essentially poetry, and poetry means action; we can scarcely appreciate a happiness that just comes our way; we want to have made it. A child is not in the least interested in our gardens, and goes about making a beautiful garden for himself with mounds of sand and bits of straw. Can you imagine a collector who did not do his own collecting?

I feel fairly certain that what we like about war is the fact that we make it. As soon as a man is armed, he obviously has a measure of liberty; and we would laugh at a field officer who tried to force his men to fight. But as soon as the men are aware of a certain freedom of action, they enter into a new way of life and develop a taste for it. We will always fear death, and wait for it, and finally submit to it. But he who goes to meet it and calls it, so to speak, into the arena, such a man feels stronger than death. Everyone knows that it is easier for soldiers to go out looking for death than to wait for it; and we prefer the destiny that we make for ourselves to the one time brings us. There is, therefore, a kind of poetry in war which even turns us away from hatred of the enemy. It is the ecstasy of freedom which makes war and all our passions understandable. A plague is imposed; a war, in a sense, is invented, like games. That is why it seems to me that prudence is not a sufficient guarantee of peace; it is out of love for justice that we put up with peace; and it is because justice is difficult to create, more difficult than a bridge or a tunnel, it is for that reason that peace will be established; for that reason alone.

3 April 1911

XLIII

Men of Action

A police commissioner is, to my mind, the happiest of men. Why? Because he is always engaged in action, always in new and unforeseen situations. Sometimes he has to combat a fire or a flood, a landslide or an avalanche; sometimes mud, dust, disease, poverty; and finally, he often has to combat anger, and sometimes rowdy enthusiasm. Thus, at every moment of his life, this happy man finds himself faced with a clearly defined problem which calls for clearly defined action. Therefore, no universally applicable rules, no red tape, no rebukes or commendations conveyed through administrative reports; he leaves all that to his bureaucratic subordinates. As for him, he is perception and action. When these two floodgates, perception and action, are opened, a river of life buoys up a man's heart and carries it along like a light feather.

Therein lies the secret of games. Playing bridge makes life flow from perception to action. Playing soccer is even better. To be confronted by a new and unforeseen situation, promptly decide on a course of action, and then follow it up immediately by action—that fully satisfies human life. What more could you possibly desire? What could you possibly fear? Time sweeps

away regrets. One often wonders what kind of inner life a robber or bandit might have. I don't believe he has any. Always
on the watch or sleeping. All his perceptive powers are focused
on what is immediately before him. That is why the idea of
punishment, or for that matter, any other idea, does not occur
to him. This blind and deaf automaton can be frightening. But
in every man, action stills the voice of conscience; such thought-
less violence may be seen in the woodcutter's swing of the axe;
it is less apparent in the actions of a statesman, but can often
be found in the effects of his actions. People would be less astonished to find man as brutal and insensitive as an axe if they
would see that he does not spare himself either. Power has no
pity, not even for itself.

Why is there war? Because in war men become engulfed in
action. Their thought is like those electric lights that dim as
soon as the streetcar starts; I mean their rational thought. This
accounts for the formidable power of action; and it is self-
justifying by virtue of the fact that it extinguishes the inner
light of reason. Thus many base passions are extinguished—all
those nurtured by meditation, such as melancholy, dissatisfac-
tion with life, or intrigue, hypocrisy, malice, or romantic love,
or refined vice. But justice, too, is extinguished in the course of
action. The police commissioner combats a riot in just the same
way he combats a flood or a fire. The rioter, too, extinguishes
his lamp. Barbarous night. That is why there were torturers
who turned the screws and judges who heard the confessions.
That is why there were galley slaves chained to their benches,
who suffered in agony and then died, while moving in rhythm
with the oars; and other men, who cracked the whip. Those
who cracked the whip thought of nothing but the whip. Any
kind of barbarism, once established, will last. A police commissioner is the happiest of men; I would not say that he is the

most useful of men. Idleness is the mother of all vices, but also of all virtues.

21 February 1910

XLIV

Diogenes

Man is happy only when he wills and invents. This may be seen in card games; it is clear from the faces that everyone is contemplating his own power to weigh the possibilities and decide; there are Caesars of contract bridge, and crossings of the Rubicon at every moment. Even in games of chance, the player has complete power to risk or not to risk; at times, he takes the plunge regardless of the risks; at other times, he abstains regardless of his hopes; he is his own master; he reigns. Desire and fear, importune counselors in ordinary matters, have no place here because of the impossibility of making predictions. Thus gambling is the passion of the proud. Those who resign themselves to earning their pay by obeying cannot even conceive of the pleasure of playing baccarat; but if they try it, they will experience, at least for a brief moment, the ecstasy of power.

All trades are enjoyable to the extent that one may exercise authority, and disagreeable to the extent that one must obey. A streetcar conductor gets less satisfaction than a bus driver. Hunting by oneself and in unrestricted territory is very enjoyable because the hunter plans his strategy, and follows or changes it without having to account for what he does, or give his reasons. The pleasure of killing when surrounded by beaters is meager in comparison; but still, a skillful marksman will enjoy the power he exercises over emotion and surprise. Thus, those who say that man seeks pleasure and flees hardship give an inaccurate picture. Man gets bored with pleasure that is simply granted to him, and much prefers the pleasure that he wins for himself; but above all, he likes to act and to conquer; he does not like to suffer, nor to submit; and so he chooses hardship with action rather than pleasure without action. The paradoxical Diogenes was fond of saying that it is hardship that is good; he meant hardship that is chosen and willingly accepted; as for hardship that is simply endured, no one likes it.

An alpinist develops his power and gives himself proofs of it; he feels and thinks it simultaneously; this superior joy illuminates the snowy landscape. But he who has taken an electric train up to the top of a famous mountain does not find the same sun. Which is why it is perfectly true that we are deceived by the prospects of pleasure; but they deceive us in two different ways; for pleasure that is handed to us never provides the joy we anticipated, whereas the pleasure of action, on the contrary, always provides more joy than we anticipated. An athlete trains for the purpose of winning the prize; but soon, through improving and overcoming difficulties, he wins another prize which is within him and which depends on him alone. And that is what the lazy man simply cannot imagine; for he sees only the hardship and the other prize; he weighs one and then the other, and cannot make up his mind; but the athlete is already at work, encouraged by the previous day's workout, and soon finds enjoyment in his own will and in his own power. Thus pleasure can be found only in work; but the lazy man does not know that, and cannot know it; or else, if he knows it by hearsay or from past experience, he cannot believe it; that is why our calculations about pleasure are always deceptive, and boredom ensues. When the thinking animal gets bored, anger is not far off. However, the boredom of being a serf seems to me less acrid than the boredom of being a master; for, however monotonous an action may be, it always involves a certain amount of directing and inventing; whereas he who has only ready-made pleasures is naturally more ill-natured. Thus the rich govern with ill humor and sadness; the worker's weakness comes from the fact that he is happier than he thinks he should be. He pretends to be ill-natured.

30 November 1922

Egoists

One of the errors of Western religions, as Auguste Comte points out, is having taught us that man, without the benefit of divine assistance, is always and irremediably an egoist. This idea has infected everything, including the concept of self-sacrifice, so that among the most widely accepted ideas, and of even the most independent thinkers, we find the strange belief that he who sacrifices himself is still seeking his own pleasure. "One man likes war; another, justice; me, I like wine." Even the anarchist is a theologian; revolt is his reaction against humiliation; it all comes out of the same barrel.

In actual fact, we ought to see that man generally prefers action to pleasure, as youth's games show so well. For, what is a soccer match if not scuffles, punches, kicks, and finally black and blue marks and bandages? But it is all ardently desired; it is all stored up in the memory; it is thought of with relish, the legs are already eager to run. And it is magnanimity that gives us pleasure, to the point of making us scorn blows, pain, and fatigue. War, which is an admirable game and which brings out in us more magnanimity than ferocity, ought to be thought of in the same way; for what is particularly ugly in war is the slavery that paves the way for it and the slavery that follows it. In short, the anomaly of war is that the best men get themselves killed while crafty men find their chance to govern in a manner contrary to justice. But here, too, our instinctive judgment tends to be wrong; and decent people like Déroulède get pleasure out of being duped.

All of that is worthy of consideration. The egoist's contempt is futile, for he wishes to subordinate magnanimous sentiments to a calculation of pleasures and pains. "You fools who love glory that is not even your own!" And Pascal, the Catholic genius, Pascal wrote these words that have only the appearance of profundity: "We lose our lives joyfully, provided that people will talk about it." This is the same man who made fun of a hunter who goes to great pains to shoot a hare that he would not want if it were given to him. Theological prejudice must be very strong to hide from human eyes the fact that man prefers action to pleasure, action that is regulated and disciplined more than any other kind, and above all, action in the name of justice. From this action comes immense pleasure, there is no doubt about it; but the error lies in believing that action seeks pleasure; for pleasure accompanies action. The pleasures of love make us forget the love of pleasure. That is how he is made, this son of the earth, god of dogs and horses.

The egoist, on the other hand, misses out on his destiny through an error of judgment. He refuses to move a finger until he sees some lovely pleasure to be had; but in this kind of calculation true pleasures are always forgotten, for true pleasures demand hardship at the outset; that is why, when prudence calculates, sorrows always win out; fear is always stronger than hope, and the egoist ends up by pondering illness, old age, and inevitable death. And his despair proves to me that he has misunderstood himself.

5 February 1913

The King Is Bored

It is good to have things a bit hard in life and not to follow a perfectly smooth path. I pity kings if they have only to desire; and the gods, if there are any around anywhere, must be somewhat neurasthenic. They say that in former times the gods took the form of travelers and went around knocking on doors; no doubt they found a bit of happiness in experiencing hunger, thirst, and the passions of love. However, as soon as they thought a bit about their power, they said to themselves that it was all only a game and that they could put an end to their desires if they so wished by abolishing time and space. All things considered, they were bored; they probably hanged themselves or drowned themselves since those days; or else they are asleep, like Sleeping Beauty. Happiness, no doubt, always presupposes some uneasiness, some passion, a sore spot that awakens us to ourselves.

It is common to have more happiness through the imagination than through a real advantage. This results from the fact that when a man has a real advantage he thinks that that's it, and sits down instead of running on ahead. There are two kinds of riches: the kind that lets us stay seated is boring; the kind that makes us happy is the one that calls for still more projects and work, like the field that a peasant coveted before finally becoming the owner; for it is power that we enjoy, not stagnant power, but power in action. The man who does nothing likes nothing. Bring him ready-made happiness and he will turn his head away like a sick man. Besides, who would not rather make music than listen to it? Difficulty is what we enjoy. Thus every time there is an obstacle in our path, the blood tingles and the fires blaze. Who would want an Olympic wreath if it could be won without effort? Nobody would. Who would want to play cards without ever running the risk of losing? Here is an old king who plays cards with his courtiers; when he loses, he gets angry, and the courtiers know it perfectly well; since the day the courtiers learned to play well, the king never loses. So now, look how he pushes the cards aside. He gets up, mounts his horse, goes out hunting; but it is a royal hunt and the game he hunts runs right up to him; deer are courtiers too.

I have known more than one king. They were little kings, with little kingdoms; kings of their families, too well loved, too flattered, too pampered, too well served. They had no opportunity to desire. Attentive eyes read their every thought. But these little Jupiters, in spite of everything, wanted to hurl thunderbolts; they invented obstacles; they forged desires for themselves and were capricious, as changeable as the sun in January; they wanted at all costs to be able to will something, and so slipped from boredom into folly. May the gods, if they did not die of boredom, never give you one of these flat kingdoms to govern; may they lead you through mountain paths; may they give you for a companion a good Andalusian mule with eyes like wells, a brow like an anvil, and who stops dead in his tracks because he sees the shadow his ears make on the road in front of him.

22 January 1908

XLVII

Aristotle

Doing and not passively accepting, that is the essence of pleasure. Just because sweets give a bit of pleasure simply by being allowed to melt in the mouth, many people would like to taste happiness in the same way, and they are mistaken. One derives little pleasure from music if one limits oneself to listening to it without ever singing; which led a clever man to say that his enjoyment of music came through his throat and not through his ears. Even the pleasure derived from admirable drawings is a passive and unsatisfactory pleasure if you are not a collector or do not occasionally daub at a canvas yourself; for then it is not merely a question of judging, but of seeking and conquering. People go to the theatre, and are more bored by it than they would like to admit; they need to create, or at least act, which is a form of creating. Everyone can recall social comedies which only the actors found enjoyable. I remember those happy weeks when I thought of nothing but a marionette theatre; but I must add that I myself carved out the usurer, the soldier, the ingenue, and the old lady, with my knife; others dressed them. I knew nothing about the audience; I left them the pleasure of acting as critics—a paltry pleasure, but still pleasure to the extent that it involved creating something. People who play cards create continually and modify the mechanical sequence of events. Don't ask someone who does not know the game if he likes to play. Politics is not boring as soon as one understands the game; but one has to learn it. It is the same in everything; one has to learn to be happy.

They say that happiness always eludes us. That is true for happiness that we have handed to us, for there is no such happiness. But the happiness we make for ourselves is not illusory. It is a learning process, and one never stops learning. The more one knows, the more one is capable of learning. Hence the pleasure of being a Latinist, which does not diminish, but rather increases with progress. The same holds true for the pleasure of being a musician. Aristotle made the startling observation that the true musician is a man who enjoys politics. "Pleasures," he said, "are signs of power." This statement is remarkable for its conciseness and for its general applicability, and it provides a clue for those who want to understand that astonishing genius, so often and so vainly refuted. The sign of real progress in any activity is the pleasure derived from it. Thus one realizes that work is the only pleasurable thing, and the only thing that fully satisfies us. I mean freely chosen work, both the result and the source of power. Once again, not passive acceptance, but action.

Everyone has seen masons building a little house for themselves in their leisure moments. How carefully each stone is chosen! The same pleasure may be derived from any trade, for the worker creates and learns continually. Apart from the fact that mechanical perfection produces boredom, it is always disastrous when the worker has no share in the finished product, and must always begin again, without possessing what he makes, without being able to utilize it to learn more. On the

contrary, it is in the succession of creative tasks, each one leading to the next, that the peasant—I mean the peasant who is
free and master of himself—finds his happiness. However, people react noisily against this kind of happiness which involves
so much work, and always because of that pernicious idea
about the enjoyment they would get from the kind of happiness that just falls in your lap. It is hardship that is good, as
Diogenes would say; the mind, however, does not easily accept this paradox; it must work it out and, once again, the
hardship involved in pondering it is what gives pleasure.

15 September 1924

XLVIII

Happy Farmers

Work is the best and the worst of all things; the best if it is
voluntary, the worst if it is servile. The work I consider most
voluntary is that which is regulated by the worker himself according to his own knowledge and experience, like that of a
carpenter making a door. But there is a difference if the door
he is making is for his own use, for then it is an enterprise with
a future; he can test the wood, and he will be very pleased
with himself to find the crack in it that he suspected was there.
We must not forget the role of intelligence in creating our
emotions, even if it does not create doors. A man is happy as
soon as he can actually follow the progress of his own work
and can continue along in the same direction with only the
work itself as his master, whose lessons are always welcome.
Better yet if a man can build the boat on which he will sail;
there is a sense of recognition every time the tiller is moved,
and all the painstaking work is appreciated. Sometimes on the
outskirts of a town you can see workers who are building their
own houses little by little in their spare time, using whatever
materials they can get hold of; a palace does not give so much
joy; even in the case of a prince, his true happiness is in having

his palace built according to his own plans; but happy above all is the man who can feel his own hammer strokes on the latch of his door. Difficulty, then, is precisely what gives pleasure; and every man prefers a difficult task which permits him to be inventive and make his own mistakes to a task that presents no problems but that must be performed according to orders. The worst job is one in which the boss comes around to meddle or interrupt. The most miserable of creatures is a housemaid when she is taken out of the kitchen to be put in the drawing room; but the most energetic of them gain authority over their tasks, and thus make their own happiness.

Farming is therefore the most pleasant kind of work when one cultivates his own field. A farmer's thoughts move continually from his work to the results, from work that has been started to work that must be done; even his profits are not as evident nor as continually before his eyes as the earth itself, adorned with the marks of man. It is an immense pleasure to ride along leisurely in a wagon over the very stones that one has laid. And a man can even do without profits if he is assured of always being able to work on the same hillside. That is why the serf attached to the land was less of a serf than others. Every menial condition is bearable as long as one can exercise authority over one's work and be assured that the job is permanent. Following these rules, it is easy to have good workmen, and even to live off the work of others. The only thing is, the master is sure to get bored; hence, gambling and show girls. It is always because of boredom and its follies that social order is disrupted.

Men of today are not much different from the Goths, the Franks, the Alemanni, and other terrifying plunderers. The essential thing for them all is avoidance of boredom. They will not become bored if they work from morning to night and are their own masters. Thus it is that when farming is widely practiced it reduces the agitation of bored people to movements that are scarcely more noticeable than the blinking of an eye. But it must be granted that assembly-line work does not provide the same advantages. Industry must be wedded to agriculture as the vine is wedded to the tree. Every factory would then be located in the country; every factory worker would own a bit of property in the sun and would cultivate it himself. This new utopia, like the chimerical Salente depicted in Fénelon's *Telemachus*, would establish an equilibrium between the restless spirit and the placid spirit. Do we not see an attempt in this direction in a railway switchman's meager garden, which grows along the side of the tracks as obstinately as grass pushes up through cracks in the pavement?

28 August 1922

XLIX

Tasks

In *The House of the Dead* Dostoevsky shows us as they really are criminals who have been condemned to hard labor; the hypocrisies of luxury, if one may call them that, no longer exist; and although there still remain the hypocrisies that are necessary for survival, basic human nature sometimes appears.

The criminals work, and often their work is useless; for example, they demolish an old boat for its wood in a country where wood costs almost nothing. They know it perfectly well; thus, all throughout the day as they are working, with no hope of any kind, they are listless, sad, and awkward. But if they are assigned work that can be done in a day, even strenuous and difficult work, they are immediately skillful, ingenious, and cheerful. They are even more so if it is a question of work that is really useful, such as shoveling snow. But these amazing pages where we find a true description without commentary must really be read. There it may be seen that useful work is in itself a pleasure; in itself, and not because of the advantages we derive from it. For example, the prisoners do a specific job energetically and cheerfully if they will be able to rest after finishing it; the idea that they will gain perhaps half an hour of rest at the end of the day encourages them to get started, and they all agree to work quickly; but once the problem of doing the work quickly is agreed to, then it is the problem of actually doing it quickly that they enjoy; and the pleasure of inventing, planning, exercising the will, and then actually doing the work, far exceeds the pleasure of the half-hour they were promising themselves, for it would still be nothing but another half-hour in prison. And I imagine that if the half-hour is bearable, it will be because of the warm memory of the task so energetically performed. The greatest human pleasure can be found, no doubt, in difficult and voluntary work done in cooperation with others, as we can easily see in games.

There are pedagogues who would make children lazy for life simply by their insistence that children be kept busy all the time; the child then becomes accustomed to working slowly, that is to say, to working badly; the result is a kind of overwhelming fatigue continually associated with work; but if you separate work and fatigue, both are pleasant. A slow, tiring kind of work is like those walks we take simply to get a little exercise and a bit of air. We are tired throughout the whole walk; once back home, we no longer feel tired; whereas in the hardest work we feel indefatigable and light-hearted; afterwards, we relax completely, and later fall into a deep sleep.

6 November 1911

L

Works

Work that is actually begun says a lot more than intentions. There are reasons for cooperating with others, and very good ones; we can clarify them and turn them over in our mind all our life and still not join a cooperative effort. But a growing cooperative is of interest to its founder; and the stones that are there waiting to be used are, in any work, sufficient reason for continuing. Happy therefore is the man who sees in the work of the previous day the marks of his own will.

It is said that men always aim for some particular thing; but I see them listless before a perfectly reasonable goal. Their imagination does not have enough force to interest them in work that has not yet taken shape. That is why we see so many things which we consider worthwhile doing and which we do not do. Our imagination deceives us in more ways than one, but primarily because we believe that the agitation it arouses in us is a harbinger of things to come; however, this sterile movement ends up where it began; the agitation is always in the present and the projects are always in the future. Whence the expression of the lazy: "I'll do it"; but the expression of a man is rather: "I'm doing it"; for it is action which contains the future. Unforeseeable is the future, and the same is true of our works; for the future which a particular work reveals to us is never the one we imagined, and is always better; but nobody can believe that; and visionaries keep on repeating that their visions are much more beautiful than the works of other men.

But notice men who are busy and happy; they all eagerly pursue work that has been started—a grocery store that is expanding, or a stamp collection; each realizes that no work is frivolous as soon as it is in progress. I see everyone tired of imagining, and eager to see stones that are waiting to be used. Embroidery is hardly enjoyable for the first few stitches; but as it progresses, it acts on our desire with accelerated power; that is why faith is the first virtue and hope only the second; for we must begin without hope, and hope will come from development and progress. Real plans can evolve only from the work itself. I do not at all believe that Michelangelo began to paint because he had all those forms in his head; when confronted with the inevitable, he said simply: "But that is not my trade." Still, he began to paint, and the forms emerged; and that is what painting is—discovering what one is doing.

It is often said that happiness flees before us like a shadow; and that is true of imaginary happiness because we never get hold of it. The happiness we derive from doing is in no way imaginary or imaginable; it is never anything but substantial; we cannot form an image of it. And, as writers know, there is no good subject; I would go even further and say that one must mistrust a good subject, approach it directly and begin to work on it in order to cut the phantom down to size, which means setting aside hope and having faith. Undo in order to redo. And this no doubt explains the astonishing differences that always exist between a novel and the actual story on which it is based. Painter, don't waste your time staring at the model's smile.

29 November 1922

Look into the Distance

I have only one thing to say to the melancholy man: "Look into the distance." He is almost always a man who reads too much. The human eye is not made for such close focusing; it is at rest when it can look into space. When you look at the stars or at the ocean's expanse, your eye is completely relaxed; once your eye is relaxed, your mind is unfettered and your stride more confident; everything within you relaxes and becomes supple, even your internal organs. But don't make a deliberate effort to relax by exerting your will power; for the will power which exists in you upsets everything when you apply it to yourself, and ends up by immobilizing you. Don't think about yourself; look into the distance.

It is true that melancholia is an illness; a doctor can sometimes determine the cause and suggest the remedy; however, this remedy, by fixing one's attention on the body and on the strict regimen to be followed, negates its own possible effectiveness; that is why the doctor, if he is wise, will send you to a philosopher. But when you consult the philosopher, what do you find? A man who reads too much, who thinks myopically, and who is sadder than you.

The state ought to establish schools of wisdom just like its schools of medicine. How could this be done? Through true science, which is the contemplation of things, and poetry as vast as the world. For the mechanism of our eyes, which relax when we view distant horizons, teaches us a profound truth. Thought must free the body and lead it back to the universe, which is our true homeland. There is a profound relationship between our human destiny and the functions of our body. An animal lies down and sleeps as soon as it is left in peace; man thinks; if his thoughts do not extend beyond himself, he is lost; then his misfortunes and needs double; fear and hope gnaw at him; consequently his body tenses and moves this way or that, backwards or forwards in agitation, according to the whims of his imagination; he becomes suspicious and mistrustful of things and people around him. And if he tries to free himself, there he is with his nose in a book—another circumscribed world too close to his eyes and too close to his passions. Thought becomes a prison, and the body suffers; for, to observe that one's thoughts have narrowed and that one's body has begun to act against itself, is to observe one and the same phenomenon. The ambitious man goes over his speeches incessantly; and the lover, his entreaties. If the body is to be healthy, thought must journey outward and contemplate.

Science will guide us to that point, provided that it is not ambitious, wordy or impatient, and provided that it turns us away from books and directs our gaze to distant horizons. What is required, therefore, is perception and outward movement. Once you begin to discover the true relationships of an object to the rest of the world, you are led to another object and then to a thousand others, and this torrent carries your thought to the winds, to the clouds, to the planets. True knowledge can never be revealed in some little object held close to the eyes; for to know is to understand how the smallest thing relates to the whole; no thing is an entity in itself, and so the movement which draws us away from ourselves is the best; it is just as healthy for the spirit as for the eyes. Thus your thought will find repose in this universe which is its domain and will be in harmony with the functions of your body, which is also bound to all things. When Christians said: "The heavens are my true home," they did not realize how true that was. Look into the distance.

15 May 1911

L I I

Traveling

In these vacation months, the world is full of people rushing from one sight to another, obviously hoping to see a great deal in a short time. If it is so they can talk about what they have seen, all well and good, for it is best to be able to mention the names of several places; that is one way of killing time. But if it is for themselves, if they really want to see something, I do not quite understand them. When you see things on the run, they all look alike. A waterfall is still a waterfall. Thus someone who travels around at full speed is hardly richer in memories at the end than at the outset.

The real richness of sights is in their details. Seeing means going over the details, stopping a little at each one, and then taking in the whole once again. I don't know if other people can do that quickly and then run off to look at something else, and start all over again. As for me, I cannot. Happy are they who live in Rouen and who every day can glance at something beautiful—the old Benedictine Abbey of Saint-Ouen, for example—as if it were a painting in their own home.

However, if you visit a museum only once or stop only briefly in one of the countries on the tourist circuit, it is almost inevitable that your memories become confused and then form a kind of gray picture with indistinct lines.

To my mind, traveling means going a few feet, then stopping and looking to get a different view of the same things. Often, going to sit down a little to the right or to the left changes everything, and a lot more than going a hundred miles.

Going from waterfall to waterfall, I always find the same waterfall. But if I go from rock to rock, the same waterfall changes at every step. And if I return to something I have already seen, it strikes me more than if it were new; and in fact it is new. To avoid getting into a rut, all one has to do is contemplate something rich and varied. It should be added that as one learns to see better, one discovers inexhaustible joys in even the most common sights. Moreover, the sky with its stars can be seen from anywhere; now there is a marvelous precipice.

29 August 1906

The Dagger Dance

Everyone knows about the strength of character of the Stoics. They reasoned on the passions—hate, jealousy, fear, despair— and thus managed to keep a tight rein on them, just as a good coachman controls his horses.

One of their arguments which I have always found good, and which has been useful to me more than once, is their concept of the past and of the future. "We have only the present to bear," they said. "Neither the past nor the future can harm us, since the one no longer exists and the other does not yet exist."

That is quite true. The past and the future exist only when we think about them; they are impressions, not realities. We go to a great deal of trouble to fabricate our regrets and our fears. I once saw a juggler pile up daggers one on top of the other so as to make a kind of monstrous tree which he balanced on his forehead. That is just the way we pile up and carry around our regrets and fears, like foolhardy performers. Instead of carrying a minute around with us, we carry around an hour; instead of carrying around an hour, we carry around a day, ten days, months, years. A person who has a pain in his leg thinks how he suffered from it yesterday, how he suffered from it before that, how he will suffer tomorrow; he bemoans his entire life. It is clear that in such a case wisdom cannot do much, for the actual suffering is still very much there. But if it is a question of moral suffering, what would remain of it if one could be cured of regretting the past and of worrying about the future?

A rejected lover, who tosses and turns in bed instead of sleeping and who plots a dreadful, Corsican revenge, what would remain of his distress if he did not think about the past or the future? The ambitious man, stung to the quick by a failure, where can he get his misery except from a past that he dredges up and from a future that he invents? One is reminded of the legendary Sisyphus who rolls his stone up the hill and thus renews his torment.

I would say to all those who torture themselves in this manner: keep your mind on the present; keep your mind on your life, which moves onward from minute to minute; one minute follows another; it is therefore possible to live as you are living, since you are alive. But the future terrifies me, you say. That is something you know nothing about. What happens is never what we expected; and as for your present suffering, you may be sure that it will diminish precisely because it is so intense. Everything changes, everything passes away. This maxim has often saddened us; the very least it can do is console us once in a while.

17 April 1908

LIV

Declamations

Sometimes one meets on the road a human specter who is warming himself in the sun or who is dragging himself home; the sight of this extreme decrepitude and imminent death immediately inspires in us an insurmountable horror; we flee from him, saying: "Why isn't that human wreck dead?" He, however, still loves life; he warms himself in the sun; he does not want to die. A hard road for our thoughts to follow; our reflections often stumble on it, are injured, get angry, rush down a wrong path. It happens quickly.

After seeing something of the kind, I was looking for the right road with careful, groping arguments, when a friend of mine appeared before me, trembling, with halting speech, and with the fires of hell in his eyes. At last he burst out: "All is misery," he said. "Those who are well fear illness and death; they set about it with all their energy; their terror does not abate; they savor every bit of it. And just look at those sick people; they ought to invoke death; but no; they repulse it; this fear adds to their misery. You say: How can one fear death when life is as horrible as that? You now see, however, that one can loathe both death and suffering; and that is how we shall all end up."

What he said seemed perfectly obvious to him; and I must say, I could believe it just as fervently as he, if I wanted to. It is not difficult to be unhappy; what is difficult is to be happy; this is no reason for not trying; on the contrary. As the proverb says, everything worthwhile is difficult.

Then too, I have reasons for mistrusting this Mephistophelian eloquence which deceives me with a false impression of being obvious. How many times have I proved to myself that I was in a desperate situation for which there was no remedy? And why? Because of a woman's eyes, dazed, tired, or perhaps darkened by a passing cloud; at the very most, because of some trivial thought, some little feeling of bad temper, some hint of vanity I thought I detected in faces or words; for we have all experienced this strange madness; and we laugh about it good-naturedly a year afterwards. I have learned from it that passion deceives us as soon as approaching tears and sobs, the stomach, the heart, the belly, violent gestures, and a futile contraction of the muscles start interfering with reasoning. Naive people are taken in by it every time; but I know that this sinister light soon goes out; I try to extinguish it immediately, and I can; all I have to do is refrain from declaiming; I know perfectly well the influence my own voice has on me; I therefore try to talk to myself very calmly, and not in the grand tragic manner. So much for the tone. I also know that illness and death are normal and natural things, and that this revolt is certainly a false and inhuman thought; for thought that is true and human, it seems to me, must always be somehow adapted to the human condition and to the natural course of things. And that is already a very good reason for not giving vent mindlessly to the groans which nourish anger and which anger nourishes. An infernal circle; but it is I who am the devil, and it is I who wield the pitchfork.

25 September 1911

LV

Jeremiads

My wish for you for the year that is beginning once again,
that is to say, for the period of time it takes the sun to climb
back up to its highest point and to descend again to its lowest,
my wish is that you do not say or even think that everything
is going from bad to worse. "This thirst for gold, this pursuit
of pleasure, this neglect of duty, this insolence of young people, these robberies and unprecedented crimes, this shameless-
ness, in short, these disjointed times, which bring us mild af-
ternoons in the middle of winter"—there you have a refrain as
old as the world of men. It means simply this: "I no longer
have the pluck or joy I had when I was twenty."

If it were only a way of saying what one feels, we could
bear this kind of talk as we bear the sadness of those who are
ill. But this kind of talk has, in itself, immense power; it in-
flates sadness, it magnifies it and covers everything with a
cloak of gloom; and thus the effect becomes the cause, as when
a child becomes frightened of his little playmate whom he
himself disguised as a lion or a bear.

It is very clear that if a man, through a natural propensity
for sadness, decorates his house as if it were a catafalque, he

will only be that much sadder, everything bitterly reminding him of his grief. The same is true for our ideas; if, in a moment of ill humor, we happen to paint a dark picture of man and of things in general, which seem to us to be in a state of decay, this picture in turn plunges us into despair; and it is often the most intelligent man who is most easily duped by himself because his declamations are coherent and seem sensible.

But worst of all, this illness is contagious; it is a kind of cholera of the spirit. I know people in whose presence one cannot say that public officials are on the whole more honest and more diligent than they used to be. People who yield to their passions are so naturally eloquent, so touchingly sincere that they easily win over the gallery; and he who wishes to see things as they really are then plays the role of a fool or of a practical joker. Thus, the jeremiad becomes established like dogma and soon is a part of polite talk.

Yesterday, a wallpaper hanger, in order to strike up a conversation, said naively: "The seasons are all mixed up. Who would ever think that we're in the middle of winter? It's just like summer out; you can't tell where you are anymore." That is what he said, even after the torrid heat of last summer which he surely must have felt along with the rest of us. But a platitude is stronger than facts. And beware of yourself, you who laugh at my wallpaper hanger; for all facts are not so clear or so present in the memory as the hot summer of 1911.

My conclusion is that joy has no authority because it is young, and because sadness is enthroned and always venerated too much. From which I conclude that we must resist sadness, not only because joy is good, which would already be a kind of reason, but because we must see things as they are, and because sadness, always eloquent, always imperious, never permits us to see in this manner.

4 January 1912

The Eloquence of Our Passions

The eloquence of our passions nearly always deceives us; by that I mean this fantasmagoria, sad or joyful, cheerful or gloomy, which our imagination unfolds depending on whether our body is rested or tired, agitated or prostrate. Quite naturally we then accuse things and other people, instead of guessing the real cause, which is often small and insignificant, and making a change in it.

At this time of year when examinations begin to loom up on the horizon, more than one student is burning the midnight oil, tiring his eyes and having continual headaches—little ills that are quickly cured by rest and sleep. But the naive student does not think of that. He notices first that he is not learning very fast, that his ideas are foggy, and that the author's thought stays on the page instead of coming to him; he becomes depressed about the difficulties of the examination and his own abilities. Then, looking back through the same fog and thinking about what he has accomplished, he sees, or thinks he sees, that he has not done anything very useful, that everything needs to be gone over again, that nothing is clear or organized in his mind. Looking now toward the future, he decides that time is short and that his work is progressing very slowly; and so he goes back to his books, his elbows on the desk and his head propped up in his hands, when he ought to go to bed and sleep. His distress hides the remedy from him; and it is precisely because he is tired that he throws himself into his work. Here he would need the profound wisdom of the Stoics, which was further elucidated by Descartes and Spinoza. He should always be mistrustful of imagination's arguments, and should surmise, on reflection, that the eloquence of his passions is operating here and refuse to be taken in, which would quickly destroy the greater part of his distress; a little headache and tiredness of the eyes is bearable and does not last; but despair is terrible and aggravates itself continually.

That is the trap of our passions. A man who is extremely angry acts out for himself a very striking, brilliantly clear tragedy in which he portrays all the wrongs of his enemy, his ruses, his preparations, his scorn, his plans for the future; he interprets everything through his anger, and his anger, in turn, is increased; he is like a painter who, in painting a picture of the Furies, terrifies himself. That is the mechanism by which anger often becomes a tempest, simply for trivial reasons that are exaggerated by the raging storm in the heart and muscles. It is clear, however, that the way to calm all this agitation is not at all by thinking like an historian and poring over the insults, the grievances, and the claims; for then everything is seen in a false light, as if in a delirium. Here again, and by reflecting, we must recognize the eloquence of our passions and refuse to be taken in. Instead of saying: "That false friend always did despise me," say: "In my present state of agitation, I can't see clearly, I can't judge clearly; I am only a tragic actor who is declaiming for his own ears." Then you will see the lights in the theatre go out for lack of an audience; and the brilliant sets will be nothing more than painted cardboard. Real wisdom; a real weapon against the poetry of injustice. Alas! We are advised and led along by second-rate moralists who only know how to work themselves up into a state of delirium and pass their illness on to others.

14 May 1913

On Despair

"No rascal," someone said, "would kill himself for something as trivial as that." It is not the first time, nor the last, that an honest man believes himself disgraced, commits suicide, and is mourned precisely by those whom he thought despised him. Concerning this drama, which will be present in our memories for a long time, I have been trying to determine just why it is that a man who wants to be just and sensible often seems to have mastered certain passions only to be attacked and overcome by others; and I have also been trying to determine by what thought such a man might possibly combat despair.

To think about a situation, pose a difficult problem, look for the answer, fail to find it, not know what to do, go over and over the same ground like a horse in training, that in itself, you will say, is torture; and then too, intelligence has thorns with which to prick us. No, that isn't it at all. As a matter of fact, one must begin by not being taken in by that error. There are many problems that we cannot understand at all; and we easily console ourselves about them. An attorney, a liquidator, or a judge can decide that a situation is hopeless, or even be unable to come to any decision at all, without losing his appetite or any sleep over it. What is harmful about inextricable thoughts is not the inextricable thoughts themselves; rather it is the struggle and rebellion against their very presence, or, if you prefer, a desire that things not be the way they are. I believe that in every impulse of passion there is rebellion against the irreparable. For example, if loving a woman who is scatterbrained, or conceited, or indifferent makes a man suffer, it is because he persists in wishing that she were not as she is. Similarly, when ruin is inevitable, and one knows it, passion persists in hoping, and, in a sense, commands thought to go over the same road once more in order to find some turnoff that might lead somewhere else. But the road has already been taken; one is where one is; and on the roads of time, one can neither turn back, nor go over the same road twice. Thus I maintain that an individual of strong character is one who tells himself where he is, what the facts are, what things are irreparable, and who then sets out from there toward the future. But this is not easy, and it must be practiced first in little things; otherwise our passions will be like a caged lion who paces in front of the iron bars for hours on end as if, when at one end, he were always hoping that he had not taken a really close look at the other end. In short, sadness which results from thinking about the past does no good at all and is even very harmful, for it makes us reflect in vain and seek in vain. Spinoza says that repentance is a second transgression.

"But," says the sad man if he has read Spinoza, "it's impossible for me to be cheerful if I'm sad; it all depends on my body fluids, how tired I feel, on my age, and on the weather." Fine. Tell that to yourself, tell it to yourself seriously; thrust your sadness back onto its true causes; it seems to me that in this way your oppressive thoughts will be dissipated, like clouds by the wind. The earth will be burdened with problems, but the sky will be clear; that is at least something gained; you will have thrust sadness back into the body; your thoughts will have been swept clean. Or let us say, if you prefer, that thought gives wings to sadness and makes of it a soaring grief; whereas, by my reflection, if my aim is good, I clip its wings, and now have nothing but a groveling grief. It is still there before my feet, but it is no longer before my eyes. Only, and here's the catch, we always want a grief that flies high.

31 October 1911

L V I I I

On Pity

There is one type of kindness that casts a gloom over life, a kindness that is sadness and that is generally called pity, one of the plagues of mankind. One has only to observe how a sympathetic woman talks to an emaciated man who is thought to have tuberculosis. The tearful eye, the tone of voice, the things that are said—everything clearly condemns this poor man. However, he does not become angry; he endures the pity of others just as he endures his illness. Thus it has always been. Everyone comes and pours out a little more sadness for him; everyone comes and sings him the same old tune: "It breaks my heart to see you like this."

There are people who are a little more sensible and a bit more careful about what they say. They give little pep talks: "Keep up your spirits; a few more days and you'll be on your feet again." But the way it is said does not seem to fit the words; it is still a mournful dirge. Even if there is only a slight nuance of pity, the sick man will sense it at once; one telling glance intercepted by him will reveal more than any spoken words.

How should one act, then? Well, one should not be sad; one

should hope; one can only give hope if one has it. One should have faith in nature, think about the future optimistically, and believe that life will triumph. This is easier than one might think, because it is natural. All living beings believe that life will triumph, otherwise they would die on the spot. This life-force will soon make you forget the poor, sick man; and it is precisely this life-force that one should give him. Really, he should not be pitied too much. It is not that we should be cruel and heartless; we should be friendly and cheerful. No one likes to inspire pity; and if a sick man sees that he does not dampen the spirits of a good-hearted man, he is encouraged and reassured. Self-confidence is a marvelous cure-all.

We have been poisoned by religion. We have become used to seeing priests spying out human weakness and human suffering so that they can smartly finish off the dying with a sermon that will inspire others to stop and think. I detest this grisly eloquence. One must preach life, not death; spread hope, not fear; and cultivate joy, man's most valuable treasure. That is the secret of the greatest of the wise, and it will be the light of tomorrow. Passions are sad. Hatred is sad. Joy destroys passions and hatred. Let us begin by telling ourselves that sadness is never noble, beautiful, or useful.

5 October 1909

The Ills of Others

The moralist—it was La Rochefoucauld, I believe—who wrote: "We always have enough strength to bear the ills of others," said something that certainly is true. But it is only half true. What is far more remarkable is that we always have enough strength to bear our own ills. And indeed we should. When necessity puts her hand on our shoulder, we are caught. Then we might as well die; or else live as best we can; and most people decide in favor of the latter. The urge to live is admirable.

Thus the flood victims adapted. They did not grumble about the footbridge; they walked out on it. Those who were crowded into schools or other public places camped there as best they could, and ate and slept wholeheartedly. Men who have been in combat say the same kind of thing; at the time, what concerns them most is not that they are in a combat situation, but that their feet are cold; they are obsessed with the idea of making a fire, and are fully content once they start getting warmed up.

It might even be said that the more difficult life is, the better one can bear hardships and the better one can enjoy pleasures; for then anticipation does not have time to go as far as those ills that are mere possibilities; it is held in check by the demands of the moment. Robinson Crusoe did not begin to miss his homeland until after he had built his house. It is no doubt for this reason that a rich man enjoys hunting; then, the ills are close at hand, such as a sore foot, and pleasures are within reach, such as a hearty meal; and action sweeps everything along, links everything together. The man who devotes his full attention to a difficult enterprise is a perfectly happy man. The man who thinks about his past or his future cannot be totally happy. As long as we carry the weight of things, we must be happy or perish; but as soon as we carry the weight of the self, every path is rocky. The past and the future are stumbling blocks in the middle of the road.

In sum, we ought not to think about ourselves. The funny thing is that it is others who lead me back to myself by their talk about themselves. To act with others is always good; to talk with others for the sake of talking, complaining, and recriminating, is one of the greatest scourges on this earth; without even taking into account that the human face is devilishly expressive, and manages to awaken feelings of sadness which other things were making me forget. Only when we are in the company of others are we egoists; this is because of the confrontation of individuals and the responses of one individual to another—responses of the mouth, of the eyes, of a sympathetic heart. A complaint unleashes a thousand complaints; one fear unleashes a thousand fears. One sheep runs and the whole flock follows. That is why a sensitive person is always a little misanthropic. These are things that friendship must always bear in mind. We would be too quick to use the word egoist if we applied it to the sensitive man who seeks solitude as a shelter from human messages; a hardhearted person does not find it difficult to bear the anxiety, the sadness, or the suffering painted on the face of a friend. And one wonders if those who voluntarily associate with misfortune are more attentive to their own ills, or more courageous, or more indifferent. That moralist was only being witty. The ills of others are hard to bear.

23 May 1910

Consolation

Happiness and unhappiness are impossible to imagine. I am not thinking of what might appropriately be called pleasure, nor of pain, like rheumatism, a toothache, or the tortures of the Inquisition; one can form an idea about such things by evoking their causes, for causes have a precise effect; for example, if boiling water falls on my hand, if I am knocked down by an automobile, if I get my hand caught in a door, in all these cases I can more or less evaluate my own pain or that of another person, at least to the extent that we are able to evaluate another person's pain.

But as soon as it is a question of the nuances of ideas which make for happiness or unhappiness, we cannot imagine them or foresee what their effect will be for others or for ourselves. Everything depends on the course of our thoughts, and we are not free to think as we wish; thus, by the same token we are able to be liberated from unpleasant thoughts without realizing how. The theatre, for example, occupies our mind and distracts us with a vehemence that is risible if we note the miserable causes—a painted canvas, a loud-mouthed oaf, a woman who pretends to weep; but these theatrics will draw tears from you, real tears; for a moment, under the influence of a tragic declamation, you will bear on your shoulders all the sorrows of man. A moment later you will be a thousand leagues from yourself and from all sorrow, journeying in distant lands. Grief and consolation are like birds that perch and fly away. One would be ashamed to admit it; one would be ashamed to say like Montesquieu: "I have never had a sorrow that an hour of reading did not dissipate"; it is clear, however, that if you read attentively, you will be completely caught up in what you read.

A man who is being taken in a cart to the guillotine is to be pitied; however, if he is thinking about something else, he is probably no sadder in his cart than I am now. If he counts the turns in the road or the bumps, he is thus thinking about the turns and the bumps. If he sees a sign from a distance and tries to read it, this might well occupy his attention at the final moment; what can we know of it? And what does he know?

I got the following story from a friend who drowned. He had fallen between a boat and the pier, and was trapped under the hull for some time; they pulled him out unconscious; he thus returned from the dead, one can rightly say. Here is what he remembers: he found himself in the water with his eyes open, and saw a cable floating in front of him; he told himself he could grab hold of it, but he had no desire to; the sight of the green water and the floating cable completely filled his thoughts. Such were his last moments, from what he told me.

26 November 1910

The Cult of the Dead

The cult of the dead is an admirable custom, and All Souls'
Day comes at the right time of year, just when it becomes
clearly noticeable that the sun is abandoning us. The withered
flowers, the red and yellow leaves underfoot, the long nights
and the lazy days which seem like evenings—everything makes
one think of weariness, of repose, of sleep, and of the past.
The end of a year is like the end of a day, like the end of a life;
since the future offers nothing but night and sleep, thought
naturally turns back to what has been, and meditates on the
past. Thus customs, the seasons, and the nature of our thoughts
are harmonized. And more than one man, at this time of year,
will summon the shades and speak to them.

But how can one summon them? How can one entice them?
Ulysses gave them food; we take them flowers; but all offerings
are only a way of turning our thoughts toward them and
starting a conversation with them. It is quite clear that what
one tries to summon is the spirit, not the body, of the dead;
and it is clear that it is within us that their spirit sleeps. This
is not to say that the flowers, the wreaths, and the decorated
graves are without meaning. Since we cannot think as we wish,

and since the course of our thoughts depends principally on what we see, hear, and touch, it is very sensible to arrange appropriate ceremonies in order to provide ourselves with the opportunity to indulge in the kinds of musings that seem to be a part of them. Therein lies the value of religious ceremonies. However, they are only a means, not an end; thus one should not visit the dead as perfunctorily as some people go to mass or say their beads.

The dead are not dead; that is clear enough since we are alive. The dead think, speak, and act; they can advise, desire, approve, criticize; that is all quite true, but one must understand in what sense. All these things are in us; all are very much alive in us.

Well then, you might say, it is impossible to forget the dead; and there is no point in thinking about them; thinking about oneself means thinking about them. True, but most people do not think much about themselves, really seriously about themselves. We are too weak and vacillating in our own eyes; we are too close to ourselves; it is not easy to get a good perspective of ourselves and at the same time keep the things around us in their proper proportions. What kind of champion of justice is a man who is obsessed with his own brand of justice? On the other hand, we see the dead as they really were, through our sense of piety which makes us forget the petty things; and their power to advise, which is perhaps the greatest human characteristic, arises from the fact that they no longer exist; for existing means having to react to the stresses of the world; it means being forced to forget more than once a day, and more than once an hour, what one was determined to be. It is, therefore, perfectly reasonable to ask oneself what it is that the dead wish. And look carefully, listen attentively; the dead want to live; they want to live in you; they want your life to develop fully what they once desired. Thus, tombs lead us back to life. Thus, our thought leaps joyfully beyond the approaching winter to the next spring and its budding leaves. Yesterday I came upon a lilac bush whose leaves were falling, and on it I saw buds.

8 November 1907

LXII

Simple Simon

People who indulge in fits of coughing with a kind of fury do so in hopes of relieving a little tickle in the throat; instead, by this splendid method they manage to irritate the throat, make themselves breathless, and become completely exhausted. That is why patients in hospitals and convalescent homes are taught to refrain from coughing; the first thing is to avoid coughing for as long as possible; better still is to swallow just at the moment one is about to cough, for it is impossible to swallow and cough at the same time; and finally one should not allow oneself to get upset or angry by that little tickle, which will subside by itself as soon as one manages to ignore it.

Similarly, there are sick people who scratch themselves in order to experience a kind of curious pleasure mingled with pain, which they later have to pay for with more intense pain. They, too, end up in a kind of rage against themselves, like those who cough with such abandon. This is Simple Simon's way of doing things.

Insomnia provides similar kinds of dramas in which we suffer from a malady that we have created for ourselves. For there is nothing wrong with lying awake for a while before going to sleep; and after all, it is not unpleasant to lie in bed. But the mind begins to work; we think about how much we want to go to sleep; we try to go to sleep; we concentrate so hard on going to sleep that we are kept awake precisely by our desire and by our concentration. Or we become irritated; we count the hours; we think it absurd to waste the precious moments of repose; all the while, we toss and turn like a fish out of water. Simple Simon's way.

Still another example, and this might happen during the day as well as at night, is the way people who are upset about something ruminate on it whenever they get a chance; they are constantly drawn back to their own unhappy tale as if it were a horror story left open on the table. They thus plunge back into their own sorrow; they wallow in it; they keep going over every detail so as not to forget a single one; they methodically run down the list of all possible misfortunes they can foresee. In a word, they scratch their wound. Simple Simon's way.

A pining lover who has been dismissed by his sweetheart does not want to think of anything else; he is preoccupied with memories of his past happiness and the charms of the faithless girl, and her perfidy, and her injustice. He tortures himself wholeheartedly. If it is simply impossible for him to think about something else, he ought at least to look at his misfortune from a different point of view: tell himself that she is a little ninny who already shows signs of wear; imagine what life would be like with her when she gets old; scrupulously examine his past joys; take into consideration the part played by his own enthusiasm; bring to mind those discordant moments that one forgets about when one is happy, but which provide consolation in sadness. Finally, he should direct his attention to one of her less attractive physical features: the eyes, the nose, the mouth, the hand, the foot, the tone of her voice; there is always at least one; I admit that this remedy requires an heroic effort. It is far easier to plunge into a difficult task, or into strenuous activity. But in any case, one must strive to console oneself instead of plunging into unhappiness as if into an abyss. And they who strive earnestly will be consoled much sooner than they think.

31 December 1911

LXIII

In the Rain

There are certainly enough real ills in the world; that does not prevent people from adding to them by letting their imagination run away with them. Every day you can meet at least one man who has complaints about his job, and what he says will seem very logical to you, for there are two sides to everything, and nothing is perfect.

You, teacher, you have to teach little savages, you say, who know nothing and are interested in nothing; you, engineer, you are up to your neck in paper work; you, lawyer, you argue your cases before judges who doze off after a heavy lunch instead of listening to you. What you say is no doubt true, and I accept it as such; there is always enough truth in such things so that you can say them in good conscience. If, in addition, you have an upset stomach, or shoes that let your feet get wet, I can understand you very well; it is enough to make you curse life, mankind, and even God, if you believe in Him.

However, keep one thing in mind: this leads nowhere, and sadness breeds sadness. For, by complaining about fate in this way, you increase your ills, you deprive yourself of all hope of being able to laugh, and even your stomach is worse off than before. If you had a friend, and if he complained bitterly about everything, you would no doubt try to calm him and make him see things differently. Why can you not be a good friend toward yourself? Yes, I seriously believe that, to some extent, one should love oneself and treat oneself with kindness. For often everything depends on the initial position we take. An author of antiquity said that every event has two handles, and that, in order to carry it, there is no sense in choosing the one that hurts the hand. Everyday language has always applied the word philosopher to those who, in all situations, choose the best and most invigorating words; which means aiming at the center. It is therefore a question of pleading in favor of ourselves, not against ourselves. We are all such good litigants, and so convincing, that we can surely find reasons for being happy, if we decide to take that road. I have often noticed that it is through carelessness and also somewhat through politeness that men complain about their jobs. If one encourages them to talk about what they are doing and what they are creating, not about what they are having to put up with, then they are poets, and joyful poets.

It starts to drizzle; you are in the street and you open your umbrella; that suffices. What is the good of saying: "This horrid rain again!"; that will have absolutely no effect on the rain, nor on the clouds, nor on the wind. Why not just as well say: "Oh! what a nice little shower!" I can hear you object that this will have absolutely no effect on the rain; that is quite true; but you will feel better for it; your whole body will awaken and actually warm up, for such is the effect of the slightest movement of joy; and there you are, able to be out in the rain without catching a cold.

And deal with men as with the rain. This is not easy to do, you say. But it is; it is much easier than dealing with the rain. For your smile has no effect on the rain, but it has a considerable effect on people and, simply by the process of imitation, it makes them already less sad and less tedious. Not to mention that you can easily find excuses for them if you look within yourself. Marcus Aurelius used to say every morning: "Today I am going to meet a vain man, a liar, an unjust man, a boring gossip; they are as they are because of their ignorance."

4 November 1907

LXIV

Effervescence

It is the same for both wars and passions. A fit of anger can never be explained by the reasons that are given in order to justify it, such as opposing interests, rivalries, malice. Favorable circumstances can always avert the tragedy. Often quarrels, brawls, murders result from a chance encounter. Let us suppose that two men from the same club, between whom an altercation seems inevitable, are obliged to take up residence, for business reasons and for a long time, in different cities that are far apart; this circumstance, so simple in itself, establishes peace between them, which reasoning would never have been able to do. Every passion is a call girl. If two people see each other every day, a tenant and his landlady, for instance, then the primary effects become, in turn, causes, and the feelings of impatience and anger are reasons for feeling these emotions even more intensely, which accounts for the fact that the primary causes and the final effect are often ridiculously disproportionate.

When a child cries or screams, a purely physical phenomenon occurs which he knows nothing about but which parents and teachers should be aware of. His crying upsets him, and irritates him still more. Threats and shouts give momentum to the avalanche. Anger itself generates his anger. Therefore, the proper response is physical—either a simple massage, or a change in perceptions. Maternal love reveals in such cases its almost infallible knowledge when a mother picks up her baby, plays with it, or rocks it to sleep. A cramp is cured by massage; anger in a baby, or in anyone, is always a state of muscular contraction that must be treated by gymnastics and music, as the ancients said. The best reasoning, however, is totally ineffectual in a fit of anger, and often harmful, for it brings back to mind everything that can excite the anger.

These remarks are helpful for understanding that war is always to be feared and can always be avoided. Always to be feared through effervescence which, if it becomes widespread, will result in war, even if the reasons are very insignificant. Always avoidable, regardless of the reasons, as long as there is no effervescence. Citizens should seriously ponder these very simple laws. For they say to themselves dejectedly: "What can I do, as just one individual, to bring peace to Europe? New causes for conflict crop up at every moment. As many insoluble problems arise as there are days that pass; a solution here causes a crisis somewhere else; untying one knot simply creates another, as in a tangled mass of string. Let's just let things take their course." All right; but their course does not have to include war, as hundreds of examples clearly show. Things can be arranged, or they can be disarranged. I saw the coast of Brittany fortified against England; however, there was no fighting in that area, despite the predictions of false prophets. But the real danger is effervescence; and here every man is his own king and master of the storms that rage within him. An immense power which the citizenry must learn to exercise. Be happy first of all, as the Wise Man said; for happiness is not the fruit of peace; happiness is peace.

9 May 1913

L X V

Epictetus

"Suppress false ideas, and you suppress evil." Thus spoke
Epictetus. The advice is good for the man who had expected
to be given the red ribbon—the one that signifies membership
in the Legion of Honor—and who is prevented from sleeping
by the thought that he did not get it. This is giving too much
power to a piece of ribbon; the man who would see it as it
really is—a bit of silk, a bit of red dye—would not be upset by
it. Epictetus abounds in harsh examples; this helpful friend
puts his arm around our shoulders: "So you're sad," he says,
"because you haven't been accorded the seat you hoped for
in the amphitheatre, and which you believe is rightfully yours.
Come then, the amphitheatre is now empty; come and touch
this wonderful stone; you can even sit down on it." The remedy for all fears and all tyrannical obsessions is the same; one
must go straight to the heart of the matter and see what is involved.

The same Epictetus said to a fellow passenger: "You are
afraid of this storm, as if you were going to have to swallow
the whole vast sea; but, my dear sir, it would take only a quart
of water to drown you." It is certain that the fearsome move-

ment of the waves misrepresents the real danger. One says and thinks: "Raging sea; voices from the abyss; angry waves; threat; onslaught." It is not true; it is a question of balancing movements which depend on weights, the tide, and the wind; no question of evil destiny; it is not the noise and movement that will kill you; no question of fate; it is possible to survive a shipwreck; it is possible to drown in calm waters; the real problem is this: Will your head be above water? I once heard a story about experienced sailors who, as they were approaching an infamous reef, lay down in the ship and covered their heads. Thus the tales they had once listened to killed them. Their bodies, washed up on that same beach, bore witness to their false ideas. He who can simply concentrate on the reef, the currents, the eddies, and, in short, on the forces that link them all together and that are perfectly understandable, that man can rid himself of all terror and perhaps of all harm. As long as we keep working, we can see only one particular danger at a time. A skillful duelist does not feel afraid, for he knows clearly what he is doing and what his opponent is doing; but if he gives himself up to chance the bad luck which is lying in wait for him will strike him before the sword does; and this fear is worse than the injury.

A man who has a kidney stone and who puts himself in the hands of a surgeon imagines how his stomach will look cut open, with rivers of blood. But the surgeon sees it differently. He knows that he is not going to cut away a single cell; that he is simply going to separate some of the cells from the colony of cells and open up a passageway; perhaps he will allow a little of the liquid in which they are bathed to flow away, no doubt less than would be lost from a poorly treated cut on the hand. He knows the true enemies of these cells, enemies against which the cells form a hard tissue that cannot easily be cut; he knows that this enemy, the microbe, is there because of the stone that blocks the excretory passages; he knows that his lancet brings life, not death; he knows that once the enemy is repelled, the whole area is soon going to live again, just as a smooth, clean cut will heal almost as quickly as it was made. If the patient forms rational ideas like these, if he suppresses false ideas, he will not thereby be cured of his kidney stone; but he will at least be cured of his fear.

10 December 1910

L X V I

Stoicism

The famous Stoics have perhaps been misunderstood, as if they had taught us only how to resist a tyrant and how to face torture bravely. As far as I am concerned, I can see more than one use for their virile wisdom, for example against rain and storms. Their thought, as is well known, consisted in dissociating themselves from a painful feeling, which they then thought of as if it were an object, saying to it: "You belong to the realm of things; you are not a part of me." In contrast, those who know nothing of the art of living like a king while sitting on a wooden stool let the storm become a part of them, saying spontaneously: "I feel the storm from afar; I yearn for it and at the same time feel overwhelmed by it. Rage then, O heavens!" This is living in an animal-like way, and thought is superfluous. For, judging from appearances, an animal reacts to an approaching storm with its whole being, just as a plant turns toward the sun, and then straightens up again in the shade; but an animal does not realize this, just as we, in a half-sleep, do not know if we are happy or sad. This torpid state is good for man, too, and is always restful, even in the worst afflictions, provided that the unhappy man relaxes completely;

I am using the word in its literal sense; the whole body must be well supported and all the muscles must become lax; there is an art in knowing how to contract them while in repose, which is a kind of internal massage, the opposite of tensing the muscles, which is the cause of anger, insomnia, and anxiety. To those who cannot go to sleep, I say without reserve: "Play dead."

And now, if one is unable to descend to this animal state, which is the essence of Epicurean virtue, then one must awaken completely and, as it were, leap all the way up to Stoic virtue; for both are good, and it is the intermediary states that are worthless. If you are unable to plunge into the stormy or rainy state, then reject it, dissociate yourself from it; say: "It is rain and storm, it is not part of me." More difficult to do, certainly, when it is a question of an unjust reproach, or a disappointment, or a feeling of jealousy; these evil creatures cling to you. But still you must finally make up your mind to say: "It's not surprising that I'm sad after this disappointment; it's natural, like rain or wind." This advice angers people who are governed by their passions; they force themselves, they create their own bonds; they embrace their woes. I like to compare them to a child who is crying his head off and gets so angry with himself when he sees how stupidly he is behaving that he cries even louder. He would be able to free himself by saying: "Come on now. It is only the child in me that is crying." But he does not yet know how to live. Moreover, most people do not know well enough the art of living. But I maintain that one of the secrets of happiness is to be indifferent to one's own ill humor; thus scorned, ill humor falls back into its animal life, as a dog goes back to his kennel. And that, to my mind, is one of the most important chapters in real ethics; dissociate oneself from one's errors, regrets, and all the miseries of reflection. Say: "My anger will pass in due time."

As in the case of a child that ceases crying, it will go away at once. George Sand, who had a good head on her shoulders, described well this kind of royal soul in *Consuelo,* a fine work not widely enough known.

13 August 1913

LXVII

Know Thyself

Yesterday I read in one of those ads of the kind you can always find: "The great secret, the sure way to succeed in life, to act upon the minds of other people, to influence them in your favor! It has to do with a vital fluid which everybody has, but which only the famous Professor X knows how to put to use. For ten francs he will teach you his secret. From now on it will be said of those who do not succeed in their enterprises that they did not have ten francs to spend, etc." Since the newspaper that prints these lines does not do it for nothing, it may be assumed that the professor of success, dealer in magnetic fluid, has his customers.

As I was reflecting on this matter, it occurred to me that the professor was no doubt much more astute than he realized. Without going into the fluid part of it, just what does he do? If he gives people a bit of self-confidence, that is already a lot; it is enough to permit his customers to triumph over the little difficulties that we tend to turn into mountains. Timidity is a great obstacle, and often is the only obstacle.

But I see something even better. I see that he trains his customers to be attentive, thoughtful, orderly, methodical, without perhaps really realizing it himself. Along with all the alleged properties of the fluid, it is always a question of having to imagine with vigor someone or something. I suppose that the professor trains them little by little until they are able to concentrate. By that alone he has well earned his money. For, first of all, by this means people are turned away from thinking about themselves, their past, their failures, their fatigue, their stomach; and there they are, rid of a burden that was getting heavier every minute. How many people waste their lives in recriminations! Secondly, they begin to think seriously about what they want, about circumstances and people, and to think clearly, instead of confusing things and harping on them, as one sometimes does in a dream. That they are then successful is not surprising. I am not even considering the strokes of good luck which work in favor of the professor. And as for the bits of bad luck, who will talk about them? In general, each of us thinks he has enemies, and we are mistaken. Men are not that consistent, and it is usual for us to cultivate our enemies more attentively than our friends. This man wishes you ill, so you think; he has no doubt already forgotten about it; but you, you do not forget; just by the expression on your face you remind him of his obligations. A man has scarcely any enemies other than himself. He is always his own worst enemy, through his false ideas, his futile fears, and the discouraging conversations he holds with himself. Simply telling a man, "Your destiny depends on you," is a piece of advice well worth ten francs; the fluid is an extra.

In Socrates' time there was at Delphi, as everyone knows, a kind of sibyl who was inspired by Apollo and who sold advice on everything. But the god, more honest than our dealer in magnetic fluid, had written his secret over the door of his temple. And when a man came to interrogate destiny in order to learn what things, favorable or unfavorable, the future would bring him, he could, before entering, read this profound oracle, applicable to everyone: "Know thyself."

29 October 1909

LXVIII

Optimism

"Let's hope that it's not the watchman," said the naive school-girls who were lost in the fields and very upset at the sight of an approaching man. More than once I pondered this example —I might almost say model—of foolishness, before understanding it in human terms. It is true that everything seems confused in it; but, no doubt, more in the words than in the ideas, as happens to all of us, for we learned to talk before learning to think.

I was reminded of this anecdote when someone quite intelligent began to stamp his foot and protest in the face of "this persistent optimism, this blind hope, this self-deception." And it was Alain he was talking about, because that naive philosopher, who is still virtually untamed, persisted in believing, despite some quite obvious evidence to the contrary, that men are basically honest, modest, sensible, and affectionate; that peace and justice come toward us hand in hand; that martial virtues will kill war; that the voter will choose the best men, and other pious consolations which, however, do not change the facts. It is exactly as if a man who intends to take a walk would say while standing on his doorstep: "Just look at that big cloud;

it's already spoiling my walk; really, I prefer to believe it won't rain." It would be better to see the cloud even blacker than it is, and take along an umbrella. He poked fun at me in this way, and I got a good laugh out of it; for such reasoning puts up a good front, but has no more depth than stage sets, and I soon got my bearings by touching the thick rustic walls which are my house.

There is a future that makes itself, and a future that we make. The real future is composed of both. As for the future that makes itself, such as a storm or an eclipse, hope is of no avail; we must understand, and observe with clear eyes. Just as we wipe the lenses of our eyeglasses, so we must wipe the mist of our passions from our eyes. I know it well: the things of the heavens, which we can never modify, have taught us resignation as well as the geometer's way of thinking, which are a good part of wisdom. But in terrestrial things, how many changes have been effected by industrious man! Fire, wheat, ships, dogs trained, horses broken in, these are works that man would not have pursued if knowledge had killed hope.

Especially in the human realm itself, where self-confidence is a factor, I would calculate very inaccurately if I did not take into account my own self-confidence. If I believe that I am going to fall, I fall; if I believe that there is nothing I can do, then I can do nothing. If I believe that my hope is deceiving me, it does then deceive me. Be wary of that. I make the good weather as well as the bad; within myself, first of all; around me too, in the world of men. For despair, and hope as well, move from one man to another faster than clouds change shape. If I trust him, he is honest; if I accuse him at the outset, he robs me. They all give me back my change according to the coin I give them. And think carefully about this too: hope is sustained only by our will power since it is based on what we shall create, if we so will it, such as peace and justice;

despair, on the other hand, settles down and strengthens itself through the power of what is. It is through such observations that we can salvage what is worth salvaging in religion, and which religion itself has lost—I mean, hope.

28 January 1913

Undoing the Knots

Yesterday someone passed judgment on me in a couple of words: "An incurable optimist." Certainly he meant it unfavorably, implying that I am that way by nature, and that I am very happy because of it, but that after all a salutary illusion has never been accepted as a truth. This is to confuse what is, with what one wishes to bring into being. If one considers simply what exists in itself without having been in any way altered by us, pessimism is truth; for the course of human affairs, as soon as one lets them go along by themselves, immediately worsens; the man who gives way to his ill humor is soon unhappy himself and nasty to others. That is inevitable because of the very structure of our body, which turns everything to ill as soon as we let down our guard, as soon as we no longer carefully control it. Notice how a group of children, when they are playing a game without rules, soon reaches the point of crude brutality. Here we can see the biological law of excitation which quickly turns into irritation. Try playing pat-a-cake with a very small child; soon he will throw himself into the game with a kind of violence that results from the action itself. Another experiment: get a young boy talking; show him just a bit of admiration; as soon as he overcomes his timidity, he will begin showing off extravagantly. The lesson will make you blush, for it is a good one, as well as a bitter one, for us all; whoever starts off talking without controlling the machine soon comes out with so many stupidities that afterwards he will curse his own nature and despair of himself. With that in mind, observe a crowd in a state of effervescence, and you will expect from it a maximum amount of evil, not to mention every possible stupidity. In this you will not be mistaken.

But he who understands evil through its causes will learn not to curse and not to despair. Awkwardness is the norm of all first attempts, in any kind of endeavor. The body that is not trained through gymnastics soon goes its own way and, whether it be sketching or fencing, horsemanship or conversation, aims poorly at first and naturally misses the mark. That astonishes us, and would seem to indicate that the pessimist is right; but to understand, we must go back to the causes, and the principal cause to consider here is the interdependence of all the muscles, which accounts for the fact that each of them, as soon as it moves, stimulates all the others and not, at the outset, the ones that are needed. An awkward person bears down with all his weight when making the slightest movement, and each of us is awkward at first, even in something so simple as pounding in a nail. However, there are no limits to the skills one can acquire through practice; all our arts and trades bear witness to it. And sketching—the outlining of our gestures—is perhaps the most eloquent witness of all, when it is beautiful; for the hand, so heavy, impatient, angry, burdened with all the feelings of the body, is nevertheless capable of such a delicate movement, so discreet and somehow purified, compliant with our ideas and at the same time faithful to the object depicted. And the man who shouts and irritates his throat is the same man who can sing; for everyone receives as a birthright a package of muscles, trembling and knotted together. We must undo the knots; and it is no small task. And everybody knows that anger and despair are the first enemies to conquer. We must believe, hope, and smile; and, in addition, work. Thus the human condition is such that if we do not accept invincible optimism as our governing standard, soon the blackest kind of pessimism becomes truth.

27 December 1921

L X X

Patience

When I go to take a train, I always hear people saying: "You won't arrive before such and such an hour. It's a terribly long, boring trip!" The unfortunate thing is that they believe it; and it is in such a case that our Stoic would be perfectly right in saying: "Suppress opinions, and you suppress evil."

If one looked at things differently, one would be led to think of a train ride as a very great pleasure. If somebody were to set up a panorama where we could see the colors of the sky and of the earth, and where things would pass before us as if on a great wheel whose center were far off on the horizon, then everyone would rush to see it. And if the inventor managed to convey the tremor of the train and all the noises of the journey, it would seem even more admirable.

As soon as you get on a train, you have all these marvels free; yes, free, because you are paying to be transported, not to see valleys, rivers, and mountains. Life is full of such vibrant pleasures which cost nothing and which we do not take advantage of often enough. There ought to be signs put up all around, and in all languages, saying: "Open your eyes, and enjoy."

To which you might answer: "I'm a traveler, not a sight-seer. An important business affair necessitates my being here or there as quickly as I can make it. That's what I'm thinking about; I'm counting the minutes and the turns of the wheels. I resent all these stops and those lethargic employees who apathetically push the baggage along. In my mind's eye, I push my own; I push the train; I push time. You tell me that this is senseless, and I say that it's normal and unavoidable if one has a little blood in his veins."

Naturally it is good to have blood in your veins; but the animals who have triumphed on this earth are not the most irascible ones; they are the sensible ones who save their passion for the right moment. Thus the most dreaded swordsman is not the one who stamps his foot and dashes forward without knowing just what he is going to do; it is the phlegmatic-looking man who waits until there is an opening and then darts through it suddenly, like a swallow. Similarly, you who are learning to do things, don't push your train since it rolls along on its own. Don't push majestic and imperturbable time, which leads all the worlds along simultaneously from one moment to the next. Things await a mere glance from you, and then they will sweep you up and carry you along. We must learn to be kind to ourselves, and to befriend ourselves.

11 December 1910

LXXI

Kindness

"How difficult it is to be pleased with another person!" This severe statement of La Bruyère should put us immediately on our guard. For common sense requires that each of us adapt to the actual conditions of life in human society, and it is not fair to condemn the average man; it is the folly of the misanthrope. Therefore, without seeking the causes, I refuse to consider my fellowmen as if I were a spectator who paid for his seat and wants to be pleased. On the contrary, going over in my mind the ordinary problems of our difficult existence, I presuppose all the worst possibilities; I assume that the man I am talking to has an upset stomach, or a migraine, or perhaps financial difficulties or family problems. A cloudy sky, I tell myself, a March sky, with blue and gray patches, periods of sunshine and a cold north wind; I have my heavy coat and my umbrella.

Good. But the mind can do better than that if we direct our attention to the unstable human body, quivering at the slightest touch, always susceptible, quickly impassioned, producing gestures and discourses in accordance with its characteristics, its degree of fatigue, and in compliance with external contingencies; it is, however, this same human body that must bring to me, like a bouquet of flowers, stable emotions, and the manifestations of respect as well as the pleasant words which, it seems to me, are my due. However, I, who am so critical of the other person, am hardly critical at all of myself; without being in the least aware of it, I send out signals by means of an unconscious gesture, for example, a frown; the sun and the wind compose my face. I therefore present to the person before me precisely what I am surprised to find in him: a man —that is to say, an animal burdened with a mind—who is always rated too high, and then too low, who cannot make one gesture without making a dozen, or rather, who conveys messages with his whole person without having chosen them. In this mixture, I must discard the gravel and the sand and, like a prospector, recognize the tiny grain of gold dust; it is up to me to look for it; no man sifts his own words as he sifts those of others. In this way I dispose myself to politeness; and even better, I make great allowances for the other person; I disregard the dross, and wait for his true thought. But at this point I observe another effect that we really do not expect often enough. The timid man who approaches me all bristling, as if he were going into combat, is soon put at ease by the kindness I show him. In short, of these two individuals moving toward each other like clouds, one of them must begin to smile; if it is not you who begin, then you are nothing but a fool.

There is no man of whom we cannot say and think many unpleasant things; there is no man of whom we cannot say and think many good things. And human nature is such that it is not afraid of displeasing; for anger, which makes us bold, follows on the heels of timidity; and the feeling that we are being unpleasant soon makes us worse. But it is up to you who have understood these things to resist getting caught up in the game. It is an amazing experiment, and I suggest that you give it a try; it is easier to control directly the emotions of others than our own; and he who cautiously handles the emotions of his interlocutor is, at the same time, doctor of his own; for in conversation as well as in the dance, each partner is the mirror of the other.

8 April 1922

Insults

If a phonograph suddenly began to hurl insults at you, you would laugh. If an ill-humored man who had lost his voice played a recording of insults to satisfy his rage, no one would believe that any particular insult, accidentally hitting the mark, had been directed specifically at him. But when it is the human face that hurls the insult, we are ready to believe that everything it says was premeditated, or at least actually thought at that particular moment. What deceives us is the eloquence of human passions and the kind of meaning that can always be read into words that were uttered with no thought behind them.

Descartes wrote the finest of his works and one too little known—*Treatise on the Passions*—precisely in order to explain how our machine, by its very structure as well as by the effects of habit, can easily disguise itself as thought. Even in our own eyes. For when we are very angry, we first imagine innumerable details which strongly reinforce our physical fury and which, by their vividness, constitute just so many proofs; and at the same time we deliver little harangues which are often full of ringing statements and verisimilitude and which move

* 195

us, the speakers, as would the art of a good actor. If someone else, imitating us, gets hot under the collar and answers us in kind, then a real drama ensues where, however, thoughts follow the words instead of preceding them. Theatrical truth resides, no doubt, in the fact that dramatic characters never stop reflecting on what they have said. Their words are like oracles in which they search for the meaning.

In a happy family, words that are improvised in the heat of impatience often reach pinnacles of ridiculousness. And we must be able to laugh at these splendid improvisations. But most people know absolutely nothing about the automatism of the emotions; they accept everything at face value, like Homer's heroes; the result is hatreds which we must call imaginary. I admire the self-confidence of a man who hates. An arbitrator scarcely listens to a witness who becomes excited to the point of rage. But as soon as a man is himself a party to a suit, he fully believes himself; he believes anything. One of our most astonishing errors is to expect anger to release a thought that has been long suppressed; that is not true even once in a thousand times; a man must be in control of himself if he is to say what he thinks. That is obvious; but impulsiveness, anger, and haste to answer back in kind will make you forget it. The good Abbot Pirard in Stendhal's *The Red and the Black* foresees what might happen: "I have a tendency," he tells his friend, "to become ill-tempered; it is possible that we shall cease speaking to each other." Naiveté can go no further. What? If my anger is caused by the phonograph—or rather bile, stomach, and throat—and if I know it, can I not boo this bad tragic actor right in the middle of his speech?

It can be assumed that curses, which are exclamations entirely devoid of meaning, were invented instinctively to permit anger a way of escaping without saying anything cutting or irreparable. And drivers in traffic jams could then be considered unsuspecting philosophers. But it is very amusing to see that among such empty cartridges, occasionally there is one that, by chance, inflicts a wound. You can insult me in Russian; I won't understand a word. But what if, just by chance, I knew Russian? Actually, every insult is gibberish. Understanding that fact is understanding that there is nothing to understand.

17 November 1913

LXXIII

Good Humor

If perchance I had to write a treatise on ethics, I would rank good humor as the first of our duties. I do not know what ferocious religion has taught us that sadness is great and beautiful, and that the wise man must meditate on death by digging his own grave. When I was ten years old, I visited the Abbey of La Trappe; I saw the graves the monks were digging a little each day, and the mortuary chapel where the dead were laid out for an entire week, for the edification of the living. These lugubrious images and the cadaveric odor haunted me for a long time; but the monks had tried to prove too much. I cannot say exactly when and for what reasons I left the Catholic Church, because I have forgotten. But from that moment on, I said to myself: "It is not possible that they have the true secret of life." My whole being rebelled against those mournful monks. And I freed myself from their religion as from an illness.

All the same, I still bear its mark. We all do. We whine too easily, and about insignificant things. And when circumstances bring us a genuine sorrow, we believe it our duty to display it. There are in circulation many false ideas on this subject, and they smack of the sacristan. A man who knows how to weep is to be forgiven anything. And so you can imagine the tragedies that are acted out in cemeteries. The orator seems crushed, and his words stick in his throat. A man of antiquity would pity us. He would say to himself: "What? That man who is speaking is not giving any consolation at all. Thus he cannot be a guide who leads men through life. He is nothing but a tragic actor; a master of sadness and death." And what would he think of the barbaric *Dies Irae?* I believe he would relegate this hymn to the domain of tragic drama. "For," he would say, "it is when I am free from sorrow that I can indulge in the spectacle of depressing emotions. Then, it is a good lesson for me. But as soon as a real sorrow strikes me, my sole duty is to act like a man and cling firmly to life; I must unite the forces of my will and my life against unhappiness, like a soldier facing the enemy; and I must speak of the dead with warm feelings and joy to the extent that I am able. But these people, with their despair, would make the dead blush, if the dead could see them."

Yes, after dismissing the lies of priests, it remains for us to live life nobly, and refrain from lacerating ourselves, and others too, by contagion and by tragic declamations. And better yet, for all things are linked, in order to counteract the little ills of life, we should refrain from talking about them, from displaying or exaggerating them. We should be kind toward others and toward ourselves. Helping others to live, helping oneself to live, that is true charity. Kindness is joy. Love is joy.

10 October 1909

L X X I V

A Cure

After they had talked about their mineral baths, their show-
ers, and their diets, someone else said: "For the last two weeks
I've been taking a good temper cure, and I'm feeling a lot better now. There are times when our thoughts turn sour, when
we rage against everything, when we see nothing beautiful or
good either in others or in ourselves. When our ideas take a
turn like that, it's time for a good temper cure. It consists in
exercising your good temper against every mishap and especially against trivial things which would set you to ranting if
you didn't happen to be taking your good temper cure. But
when you are, then, on the contrary, these little annoyances
are very useful, just as hills are good for building up your leg
muscles.

"There are boring people," the same person continued, "who
meet together for the sole purpose of recriminating and complaining; under ordinary circumstances, you would flee from
them; but during your good temper cure you do the opposite,
and seek them out; they're like those arm exercisers you can
use in order to keep in shape at home. After starting out by
pulling the smallest ones, you finally manage to stretch out

the biggest ones. In the same way, I rank my friends and acquaintances according to their level of ill humor, and practice on them in ascending order, one after the other. When they are even more sour than usual, more adept at spitting in every platter, I say to myself: 'Ah! Here's a real test! Have courage, heart; go to it; try and lift up that burden of woe.'

"Things," the man continued, "are often good enough—I mean bad enough—for a good temper cure. A burned stew, stale bread, the sun, dust, accounts to balance, an almost empty pocket, these provide occasions for valuable exercise. You say to yourself, as in boxing or fencing: 'Here comes a masterly blow; I've got to ward it off, or else take my punishment.' Under ordinary circumstances, you begin to yell like a child, and are so ashamed of yelling that you yell still harder. But during a good temper cure, things are entirely different; you accept the situation, whatever it is, as you would a good shower; you move your body; you shrug your shoulders rhythmically; then you stretch your muscles and make them supple, flexing them against each other like laundry swishing in a tub; then a rush of life flows through you just as water flows down a stream that has been undammed; your appetite returns; the washing has been done, and life feels good. But I must leave," he said; "your faces are now beaming; you are no longer of any use to me in my good temper cure."

24 September 1911

Mental Hygiene

Yesterday I was reading an article about certain kinds of mad-men who have fixed ideas and who, by dint of always seeing things from the same angle, end up by believing themselves persecuted, and soon become dangerous and have to be locked up. This article, which plunged me into sad thoughts (what can be sadder to think about than a madman?), re-minded me, however, of a good retort I once heard. Someone was talking about a man who was obsessed almost to madness by the idea that he was persecuted and who, in addition to everything else, always had cold feet; a wise man who hap-pened to be present said: "Poor circulation of the blood, and poor circulation of ideas." These words merit some thought.

It is certain that each of us has any number of crazy thoughts, such as dreams or a ludicrous association of images. It is our internal language in particular which stumbles and which, because of a mistake in pronunciation, often plunges us into some absurd idea. But we do not keep going over and over it. In the normal man there is a continual change of ideas, like the continual changes in the flight of gnats. And we forget all our absurdities so thoroughly that we would never be able to answer precisely the following question which seems so simple: "What are you thinking about?" This circulation of ideas often leads to a certain futility and puerility. However, it is the very thing that makes the mind healthy. And if I had to choose, I would rather be insouciant than obsessed.

I do not know if people who teach children and adults have given that idea sufficient thought. To hear them tell it, we are led to believe that the main thing is to have ideas that are firmly cemented together and very heavy to move. To which they accustom us early in life with their ridiculous memory exercises; and all the rest of our life we drag along rosaries of bad verses and hollow maxims that make us stumble at every step. Later, they shut us up in some specialty that has its own litany. They train us to chew the same fodder over and over again. And that becomes dangerous with age, as our thoughts tend to become bitter. We recite our sadness mentally, just as we recite the rhymes we memorized to learn geography.

On the contrary, let us unknot our minds. I would give as a rule of hygiene: "Never have the same thought twice." To which the hypochondriac will say: "I can't help it; that's the way my brain is made, and my blood circulates through it at its own speed." Of course. But we know of a way of massaging the brain; all you have to do is change your ideas; and it is not difficult if you have practiced it. There are two infallible ways of purging the brain. One consists in looking around yourself and taking a kind of shower of sights; it never fails. The other consists in going back from effects to causes, which is a sure way of driving out black thoughts. For, following the chain that leads back from effect to cause is a journey, and soon we are very far away; it is another way of interrogating the oracle, as if, instead of looking for the reasons why Pythia prophesied that I would end up as a miser, I tried to understand how her mouth had formed that particular word rather than another; there I am, thinking about vowels and consonants, following the natural propensity that leads us from one to the other; the whole of phonetics comes into the picture. Someone I know had had a rather frightening dream. When I suggested that he look for its true causes, which may often be found in perceptions combined with little discomforts, he launched into various hypotheses, and I saw that he was freed. Circulation was reestablished.

9 October 1909

A Hymn to Milk

I find in Descartes the idea that love is good for the health, and that hate, on the other hand, is bad. An idea that is known, but not familiar enough to all of us. To be more precise, we do not believe it. And if Descartes were not almost as far above mockery as is Homer or the Bible, we would find it risible. However, it would be no small step in the direction of progress if people were to decide to do in love everything they do in hate, choosing from among those composite things called men, actions, and works, always what is beautiful and worthy of love; and that is the most effective way of deprecating what is bad. In short, it is better, it is fairer and more effective to applaud good music than to hiss bad music. Why? Because love is physiologically strong, and hate, physiologically weak. But it is characteristic of people who yield to their passions not to believe a word of what is written about our passions.

In order to understand, therefore, we must get at the causes; and I find these causes, too, in Descartes. For what is our first love, he asked, our oldest love, if not our love for our blood enriched by nourishing food, for pure air, for gentle warmth, in sum, for everything which makes a baby grow? It is in our earliest years that we learned the language of love, which at first was love of self expressed through the movement, flexion, and delightful harmony of the vital organs as they welcomed the good milk. The nodding of our head saying yes to a good soup was exactly like that first approbation. And notice how, in contrast, the head and indeed the whole body of a child say no to a soup that is too hot. Similarly, the stomach, the heart, and the entire body say no to any food that is harmful, and even to the point of rejecting it by vomiting, which is the most energetic and the oldest expression of contempt, disapproval, and aversion. That is why Descartes, with Homeric conciseness and simplicity, said that hatred in a man impedes digestion.

One can expand and develop this admirable idea; one cannot exhaust it, for it is limitless. The first hymn of love was this hymn to maternal milk, sung by the infant's whole body, welcoming, embracing, taking in its fill of the precious nourishment. And this joy in suckling is physiologically his first pleasure in the world. Who does not recognize that the first example of a kiss can be found in the suckling infant? A man never forgets this first act of piety; he later kisses the cross. For what we communicate must necessarily have its origin in our body. And similarly, the impulse to imprecate is the ancient action of the lungs refusing foul air, of the stomach rejecting sour milk, of all the body's tissues mobilizing for defense. What benefit can you hope to derive from your dinner, O imprudent reader, if your food is seasoned with hatred? Why do you not read Descartes' *Treatise on the Passions of the Soul*? It is true that your bookseller has never even heard of it, and that your psychiatrist does not know about it either. Knowing how to read is almost everything.

21 January 1924

Friendship

There are marvelous joys in friendship. This is easily understood as soon as one realizes that joy is contagious. If my presence gives a friend some real happiness, the sight of his happiness is enough to make me in turn feel happy; thus the joy that each of us gives is returned to him; at the same time, vast reserves of joy are released; both friends say to themselves: "I had happiness in me that I wasn't making use of."

The source of happiness is within us, I'll admit that; and there is nothing sadder to see than people dissatisfied with themselves and with everything else, and who have to tickle each other in order to be able to laugh. However, it must be added that a happy man quickly forgets that he is happy once he is alone; all his joy soon becomes numbed; he sinks into a kind of unawareness bordering on stupor. An inner feeling needs an external form of manifestation. If some tyrant or other imprisoned me in order to teach me respect for the mighty, I would make it a rule of good health to laugh every day all alone; I would exercise my joy just as I would exercise my legs.

Here is a bundle of dry branches. They seem as inert as

earth; if you leave them there, they will become earth. However, locked within them is a hidden ardor which they captured from the sun. Bring the smallest flame near them and soon you will have a crackling fire. All you had to do was rattle the door and awaken the prisoner.

In the same way, there must be a kind of starting signal to awaken joy. When a baby laughs for the first time, his laughter expresses nothing at all; he is not laughing because he is happy; instead, I should say that he is happy because he is laughing; he enjoys laughing, just as he enjoys eating, but first he has to try eating. This is not only true for laughter; one needs words in order to know what one is thinking. As long as one is alone, one cannot be oneself. Simple-minded moralists say that loving means forgetting yourself; that is too simplistic; the more you get away from yourself, the more you are yourself; and the more you feel alive. Don't let your wood rot in the cellar.

27 December 1907

On Irresolution

Descartes says that irresolution is the greatest of all evils. He says it more than once, but never explains what he means. I know of no greater insight into the nature of man. All our passions and their sterile agitations may be explained by it. We like games of chance, whose influence over our souls is so imperfectly understood, because they involve the power of making decisions. They are a kind of challenge hurled at the nature of things, making everything nearly equal and unceasingly nurturing even our least significant deliberations. In a game of chance, all possibilities are absolutely equal, and one must choose. This abstract risk is like an insult to thought; one must simply make a choice. From then on, the game takes over; and one cannot have any of those regrets which poison our thoughts; one cannot, because there was no reasoning involved. One cannot say: "If only I had known," since not knowing is the fundamental rule of the game. It does not surprise me that the only remedy for boredom is gambling; for boredom is principally a matter of deliberating while knowing that your deliberations will lead nowhere.

One might wonder what causes the suffering of a man in

love who cannot sleep, or of an ambitious man who has been disappointed. This kind of suffering is entirely in the mind, although one could also say that it is entirely in the body. The agitation which drives away sleep is the result of futile resolutions which decide nothing, and which invariably produce a physical reaction, making the body jump like a fish out of water. There is violence in irresolution: "That's that; I'll not tolerate any more"; but the mind soon thinks up various ways of arranging things. One imagines the consequences of this or that decision, and no progress at all is made. The advantage of real action is that the choice which has been rejected is soon forgotten; or, more accurately, it no longer exists, because action has changed the whole situation. But to simply envisage an act is nothing, and everything remains the same. There is an element of gambling in every action; for action cuts off deliberations before they have exhausted their subject.

I have often thought that fear, which is naked passion and the most painful kind, is simply the feeling of what I might call muscular irresolution. One feels called upon to act, and yet feels incapable of doing anything. Dizziness affords an even clearer picture of fear, because suffering here is caused only by a doubt that cannot be overcome. It is always because of too much mental activity that one suffers from fear. Certainly the worst thing in afflictions of this kind—and the same holds true for boredom—is that we imagine we are incapable of freeing ourselves from them. We think of ourselves as automatons, and we despise ourselves. The essence of Descartes is contained in that sovereign statement which reveals causes and the remedy as well. A martial virtue; and I understand Descartes' desire to experience military life. Marshal Turenne was always on the move, and thus cured himself of the evil of irresolution which he then inflicted on the enemy.

Descartes did the same thing in the world of the mind; bold

in his thoughts and always proceeding with sovereign authority, always making decisions. Irresolution in a geometer would
be profoundly comic, because it would be infinite. How many
points are there in a line? What does the mind really understand of its perception of two parallel lines? But the genius of
the geometer lies in his decision that such things are known,
and he vows not to change his mind or to go back over the
problem. If you carefully examine a theory, you will see that
it is made up of nothing more than errors precisely stated and
attested to as fact. In such a game, the power of the mind resides in never thinking that it has formulated a fact, when it
has merely made a decision. Therein lies the secret of always
being confident without ever believing anything. It has been
resolved; there is an admirable expression, and with a double
meaning.

10 August 1924

LXXIX

Ceremonies

If irresolution is the worst of all evils, then we can understand why ceremonies, social functions, formal attire, and fashions are the gods of this world. Every time we are required to improvise, we become upset, not so much because of the idea of what we could do or say differently, but rather because of the combination of two reactions in the body, disorienting our servants, the muscles, and quickly thereafter, the heart, our tyrant. A man who has been surprised and put on his guard is a sick man. That is why freedom makes man ill-willed. A child shows this; there is no game without rules that does not tend to become brutal. On this point we would be badly mistaken if we were to infer the existence of evil instincts which are always bent and ready for use, like bows, and which are repressed by laws. For we like laws; the absence of laws, on the other hand, displeases and irritates us because of the resulting irresolution, causing us to rush into folly. Man, naked, is frenzied. Clothing is already a law, and every law gives pleasure, just as does clothing. Louis XIV exerted an authority over those who drew near him that was astonishing and, on the surface, inexplicable; it resulted from the many laws he established, governing every facet of his daily activity—his getting up, his going to bed, his use of the chamber pot. One cannot say that he imposed these laws because he was powerful; on the contrary, he had power because he was himself the law; everyone around him always knew at every moment exactly what was expected of him; which brings to mind the serenity of Egyptian statuary.

There is every reason for disliking war; but here our reasoning is mistaken; the truth is that men quickly find peace in war; I mean real peace, the kind that dwells within us. In war everyone knows what he has to do. Reason vainly evokes danger, but does not terrify; it cannot manage to cover up a persistent light-heartedness; everyone has a well-defined function which is his lot, and things to do that he cannot put off; all his thoughts rush toward them, and the body follows; and this consensus of thought and action soon leads to a state of human affairs that must be endured, as one endures a cyclone. We are astonished at how much the powerful can obtain; but they obtain much precisely because they demand much. Monastic rule, which cures irresolution so effectively, works on the same principle. It is inadequate simply to recommend prayer; one must require that a particular prayer be said at a particular hour. The wisdom of the powerful always consists in giving a sharp command with no explanation. Any sort of explanation would quickly give rise to a couple of thoughts, and then a hundred. Certainly thinking is pleasant; but the pleasure of thinking must be subordinated to the art of making decisions. It is in Descartes that we can see the model of this type of man; and we know that he took part in military campaigns, not for pleasure, but as a means of freeing himself from thoughts that touched him too deeply.

We would like to make fun of fashion; but fashion is a very serious thing. A man pretends to despise it, but first he puts on a necktie. The uniform and the cowl are surprisingly effective in calming us. They are garments of sleep; they are the apparel of idleness, of the sweetest idleness, the kind that acts without thinking. Fashion aims at the same goal, but it allows the pleasure of a certain amount of choice, which takes place entirely in the imagination. Colors attract, but the necessity of choosing would be frightening. Here, the evil is shown only so that we can better enjoy the remedy, just as in the theatre. Hence, security yesterday was in red, and today, in blue. It is an agreement of opinion, and such an agreement constitutes proof. The result is a feeling of serenity which really does improve appearances. For it is true that yellow is not becoming to blonds, nor green to brunettes. But the grimace of anxiety, of desire and regret is becoming to no one.

26 September 1923

Happy New Year

All these gifts during the holiday season succeed in stirring up more sadness than joy. For no one is rich enough to start the new year without doing a lot of calculating; and more than one man will secretly bemoan the white elephants he got from this or that person, and those he gave to this or that person, thereby enriching the merchants. I can still hear the little girl whose parents had many friends and who said, seeing the first ink blotter she got that season: "Uh huh, here come the ink blotters." There is a lot of indifference, and also repressed anger, in this fury of giving. Obligation spoils everything. And the chocolate bonbons burden the stomach and nourish our misanthropy at one and the same time. Bah! Give quickly, and eat quickly; it's just something you have to get through.

Let's get down to serious matters. I wish you good humor. That is what we should give and receive. That is the true politeness which enriches everybody, and first of all, the giver. That is the treasure which grows as it is exchanged. One can strew it along the streets, in streetcars, around newspaper stands; not one particle of it will be lost. It will grow and flourish wherever you have sown it. When, at some intersection, there is a tangle of carriages, then all you can hear are curses and invectives, and the horses tug with all their might, making a bad situation even worse. Every difficulty is like this; easy to untangle if one would smile, moderate his actions, bring a bit of calm to the rage that shouts gee and haw; but in contrast, it will become a Gordian knot if, with clenched teeth, one pulls on every cord. The lady of the house, who is late, clenches her teeth; the cook clenches her teeth; the leg of lamb is probably overcooked; furious tirades will ensue. All these Prometheuses would have been unbound and freed if someone had only smiled at the right moment. But no one thinks of such a simple thing. Everyone does his best to pull on the cord that is strangling him.

Life with other people multiplies the difficulties. You enter a restaurant. You cast a hostile glance at the person next to you, another at the menu, another at the waiter. That does it. Ill humor rushes from one face to another; around you everything goes awry; perhaps there will be broken glasses, and the waiter will beat his wife that night. But try to understand this mechanism and this contagion; and there you are, a magician and provider of joy, a beneficent god everywhere you go. Say a good word, a warm thank you; be charitable about the cold veal; you can ride this wave of good humor to the smallest beaches; the waiter will call in your order in a different tone of voice, and people will move among the tables differently; thus the wave of good humor will spread out around you, buoying up everything, including you. This has no bounds. But pay close attention to the way you start off. Begin the day well, and begin the year well. What an uproar in this narrow street! What inconsiderateness, and what violence! Blood flows; the whole thing will end up in court. All this could have been avoided by the prudence of just one coachman, by just a slight movement of his hands. So, be a good coachman. Put yourself at ease on your seat, and keep a firm hold on your horse.

8 January 1910

Good Wishes

All these greetings and all these good wishes—January blooms —are only signs; agreed. But signs are very important. Men have lived centuries upon centuries believing in signs, as if the whole universe, by means of clouds, thunder, and birds, wished them good hunting or augured a bad journey. The universe does not announce just one specific thing after another; and the error consisted in simply interpreting this world as if it were a face which registered approval or criticism. We are fairly well cured of wondering whether the universe has an opinion, and what it might be. But we will never be cured of wondering whether our fellowmen have an opinion, and what it might be. We will never be cured of it, because this opinion, as soon as it is indicated by some sign, profoundly changes our own.

Something worth noting: we feel that we are stronger against an opinion that is supported by reasons and explicitly stated than against an unexpressed opinion. The first kind of opinion, which is advice, we often hold in contempt; the other kind, we cannot scorn. It takes hold of us more profoundly; and since we do not know exactly how it takes hold of us, we

cannot free ourselves from it. There are faces that express a kind of constant criticism of everything. In such cases, flee if you can. For man imitates man; and there I am, by the movements of my face and without my being able to realize it, there I am, beginning to criticize too. Criticize what? I have no idea. But this sad outlook colors all my ideas and all my plans. I look for the explanation in these very ideas and in these plans. I look for the explanation and I always find one, for everything is complicated, and there are dangers everywhere. And since one must, after all, act and brave the dangers, even if it is nothing more than crossing the street, I act without confidence, that is to say, less spontaneously, less freely. A man who has the idea that he is going to get run over is not helped by that idea; instead, he is paralyzed. In matters that take longer and are more involved and uncertain, the effect of the forebodings we get from a hostile face is still more pronounced. A certain kind of glance will always cast a spell over us.

But let's go back to this festival of politeness, which is an important festival. During this holiday season when each of us looks at the future imprinted on the cards that the mailman brings, it would be very bad if the coming weeks and months, about which we can know nothing for certain, were tinged with the hue of sadness. It is a good custom, then, that on New Year's Day each of us be a prophet of happiness and raise the colors of friendship. A banner flying in the wind can gladden a man's heart; he knows nothing about the other man's mood, the one who hoisted the banner. Better yet: this joy expressed on faces is good for everyone; particularly when it is expressed on the faces of people I hardly know; for then I do not discuss the signs; I take them at face value; that is the best way. And it is profoundly true that a sign of joyfulness predisposes to joy the very person who initiates it, especially since these signs are reflected back to us unceasingly by the process of imitation. Do not say that the joy of children is childish. Even without thinking, even without the least affection, we pay a great deal of attention to the signs of children; here everyone is a nursemaid; here everyone initiates the game of imitating for the purpose of understanding, which is how we teach children.

This holiday will be good for you, whether you want it to be or not. But if you want it to be, if you consider the admirable concept of politeness from every angle, then this day of festivity will really be a festive day for you. For, predisposing your thoughts in accordance with the idea of signs, you will make a firm resolution never to convey a baneful sign in the coming months, nor any omen that might decrease another person's joy; in this way, you will first of all be made strong against all the little ills which are really nothing, but which become something through our tragic declamations. And your hope for happiness will make you happy at once. That is my wish for you.

20 December 1926

LXXXII

Politeness

Politeness is learned, like dancing. He who does not know how to dance thinks that the difficult part is learning the rules of dancing and making his movements conform to them; this is only a superficial view of the matter; one must be able to dance without stiffness or awkwardness, and therefore without fear. In just the same way, learning the rules of politeness is only a small part of it; and even if you obey them, you are still only on the threshold of politeness. Your movements must be precise and supple, without stiffness or uneasiness; for the least uneasiness can be passed on to others. What kind of politeness is it if it makes other people uneasy?

I have often noticed a tone of voice which in itself is impolite; a singing teacher would say that the throat is tense and the shoulders not relaxed enough. The way you move your shoulders can make a polite gesture seem impolite. Overacted; false assurance; too forceful. Fencing masters always say: "Too much effort"; and fencing is a form of politeness which easily leads to politeness in everything. Anything that smacks of brutality and impetuosity is impolite; a hint of either is too much; the slightest threat is too much. One might say that impoliteness is always a kind of threat. Feminine sensibilities withdraw before the threat of impoliteness and seek protection. If a man's self-discipline is so weak that he cannot prevent himself from trembling, what might he say if he becomes excited and gets carried away? That is why one must not raise one's voice. Those who saw Jaurès in a drawing room had before them a man who cared little about public opinion or social customs, and whose necktie was often badly tied; but his voice emanated politeness by a melodious sweetness in which the ear sensed no forced note—something of a miracle, since everyone remembered his ringing oratory and his roaring, the voice of a lion of the masses. Strength is not incompatible with politeness; they complement each other; they represent one form of power added to another.

An impolite man is impolite even when he is alone; too much effort in the slightest movement. One senses the knotted emotions and the timidity, which is fear of self. I remember hearing a timid man publicly discuss grammar; his voice expressed the most intense hatred. And, since passions are more contagious than illnesses, I am never surprised to find people expressing themselves violently on even the most innocent topics of conversation; often this violence is only a kind of fear which is increased by the sound of one's own voice and by the futile efforts to get control of oneself. And it is possible that fanaticism starts out as impoliteness; for what one expresses, even without really wanting to, one inevitably ends up feeling. Thus, fanaticism might well be a product of timidity, a fear of not being able to uphold what one believes; and since fear cannot be endured for long, it leads to hatred directed against oneself and against everyone else, which gives formidable power to even the most questionable ideas. Look at timid people and notice how they make a decision, and you will see that all their hand-wringing is certainly a strange way to go about thinking. In this roundabout way, we can now understand how holding a cup of tea civilizes a man. Fencing masters used to size up a fencer by the way he handled his spoon while stirring a cup of coffee, with no unnecessary movements.

6 January 1922

Good Manners

There is a courtier's politeness, which is not attractive. But then too, it is not really politeness. And it seems to me that anything contrived is outside the realm of politeness. For example, a genuinely polite man can deal harshly and to the point of violence with a man who is contemptible or vicious; that is not impoliteness. Deliberate kindness is not politeness either; and calculated flattery is not politeness. Politeness refers only to the things we do without thinking, and which express something we do not deliberately intend to express.

An impulsive man, who says the first thing that comes into his mind, who gives way to his emotions, who unreservedly shows astonishment, distaste, pleasure, even before knowing what he feels, is an impolite man; he will always have a lot of apologizing to do, because he will have upset and disturbed others without intending to, and even contrary to his intentions.

It is painful to hurt someone unintentionally by speaking thoughtlessly; the polite man is he who feels the discomfort before amends become impossible, and who deftly changes direction; but there is a still greater degree of politeness in sensing at the outset what should and should not be said and, when in doubt, leaving the course of the conversation up to the host. All this in order to avoid doing harm without meaning to; for, if one deems it necessary to prick a dangerous individual in a sensitive spot, that is up to him; but properly speaking, such an act has moral implications and has nothing to do with politeness.

Impoliteness is a form of awkwardness. It is unkind to make someone feel his age; but if it is done unintentionally, by a gesture, or a facial expression, or a careless word, then it is impoliteness. Stepping on someone's foot is an act of violence if it is done deliberately; if done unintentionally, it is impoliteness. Acts of impoliteness ricochet back to us unexpectedly; a polite man avoids them and strikes only where he wants to strike; and he strikes all the better for it. Politeness does not necessarily mean flattery.

Thus politeness is a habit and a form of naturalness. The impolite man does something different from what he wants to do, like a person who knocks over china or knickknacks; he says something different from what he means; by his brusque tone, his unnecessarily loud voice, hesitation, and stammering, he communicates something different from what he wants to communicate. Politeness can thus be learned, like fencing. A fop is a man whose contrived extravagance communicates something without his realizing it. A timid man is a person who would like to be a fop, but who does not know how to go about it, for he has noticed the importance of acts and of words; and so you will see him straining and tensing to prevent himself from acting or speaking; he makes a prodigious effort to control himself, with the result that he ends up trembling, sweating, and flushed, even more awkward than he naturally would have been. Grace, on the other hand, is a harmony of expression and movement that upsets and wounds no one. And personal qualities of this kind are very important for happiness. An Art of Living must not neglect them.

21 March 1911

* 225

LXXXIV

Giving Pleasure

I spoke of an Art of Living that should be taught. As one of
the rules I would set down the following: "Give pleasure." It
was proposed to me by a man whom I had known to be rather
brusque in his ways, and who had reformed his character.
Such a rule seems astonishing at first. Giving pleasure? Does
that not mean being a liar, a flatterer, a courtier? Let us fully
understand the rule; it is a question of giving pleasure whenever possible without lies or baseness. And that is nearly always possible for us to do. Telling an unpleasant truth, with
an acid voice and a flushed face is only a gesture of ill humor,
only a brief malady that we do not know how to treat; in vain
we later try to see in it an act of courage; but that would be
highly improbable unless we had risked a great deal and, above
all, unless we had deliberated beforehand. From which I would
draw the following moral principle: "Never be insolent unless it
is a deliberate decision, and only toward a man more powerful
than yourself." But, no doubt, it is better to tell a truth without forcing the tone, and even to choose in the truth itself that
part which is praiseworthy.

There is something that can be praised in almost everything;

for we are always ignorant of the true motives, and there is no harm in supposing moderation rather than cowardice, friendship rather than cautiousness. Especially with young people, give them the benefit of the doubt in what is only supposition, present them with a handsome portrait of themselves; they will believe they are like that; soon they will be like that; criticism, on the other hand, never does any good. For example, if someone is a poet, pick out and quote his best lines; if he is interested in politics, praise him for all the harm he has not done.

I am reminded of an incident that took place in a kindergarten. A little scamp, who previously had done nothing but scribble and act silly, one day completed a third of a page in his penmanship book, and did it very neatly. The teacher went up and down the rows giving good marks; when she passed by without even noticing this third of a page done with so much effort, "Aw s. . . ," said the little scamp; his language was crude, for this school is not located in the faubourg Saint-Germain. Whereupon, the teacher came back to him and, without comment, gave him a good mark; she was grading penmanship, not fine language.

But these are difficult cases. There are so many others where one can always, without hesitation, smile and be polite and considerate. If you are jostled a bit in a crowd, make it a rule to laugh about it; laughter puts a stop to the jostling, for everyone is ashamed of the little fits of anger he has had. And perhaps you yourself will escape a serious fit of anger, that is to say, a minor illness.

That is how I would conceive of politeness; it is simply a kind of gymnastics directed against our passions. Being polite is saying or indicating by all our gestures and all our words: "Let's not get upset; let's not spoil this moment of our lives." Is it, then, evangelical goodness? No. I would not go so far as to say that; goodness is sometimes indiscreet and can cause humiliation. True politeness, in contrast, is a contagious joy that alleviates friction of any kind. And this politeness is scarcely ever taught. In what is called polite society, I have seen many a bent back, but I have never seen a polite man.

8 March 1911

Plato as Doctor

Gymnastics and music were the two great methods of Plato, the doctor. Gymnastics means regulated exercise of the muscles for the purpose of stretching and massaging them internally in accordance with their various functions. Aching muscles are like dirty sponges; we clean muscles as we do sponges, by letting them absorb liquid and then squeezing them several times. Physiologists have repeatedly told us that the heart is a hollow muscle; but, since the muscles contain a rich network of blood vessels which are alternately compressed and expanded by contraction and relaxation, one might also say that each muscle is a kind of spongy heart whose movements, a precious resource for us, can be regulated by our will. Therefore, we can see that people who have not mastered their muscles by means of gymnastics, and whom we call the timid, feel within themselves uncontrollable waves of blood flowing toward the most susceptible parts of the body; this accounts for the fact that their faces redden for no apparent reason, or too much blood rushes to their head, causing brief periods of delirium, or to their stomach, causing a discomfort that is quite common; for such conditions, methodical exercising of the muscles is assuredly the best remedy. And it is here that we see music enter the picture in the form of a dancing master who, with his little fiddle, can very nicely regulate the blood circulation in our viscera. Thus, dancing can cure us of timidity, as everybody knows; but it can also relieve the heart in another way—by stretching the muscles gently and without sudden jolts.

Someone who suffered from headaches told me recently that the movement involved in chewing his food brought him quick relief. I told him: "Then you ought to chew gum, like the Americans." But I don't know if he gave it a try. Pain plunges us immediately into metaphysical thoughts; we imagine an evil at the source of the pain, a fantastic creature who has slipped under our skin and whom we would like to exorcise by magic. It seems unlikely to us that a methodical movement of the muscles can efface pain, the gnawing monster; but generally there is no gnawing monster or anything like one; these are bad metaphors. Try to stand for a long time on just one foot, and you will notice that it does not take a great change in position to produce a keen pain, nor a great change to relieve it. In all cases, or almost all, one needs to invent a suitable dance. Everyone knows that it is a pleasure to stretch his muscles and to yawn freely; but it does not occur to anyone to try to do it through gymnastics, just to get the liberating movement going. And people who cannot get to sleep ought to mime sleepiness and the pleasure of relaxing. But, on the contrary, they mime impatience, anxiety, anger. Here are the roots of pride, which is always too severely punished. That is why, borrowing Hippocrates' bonnet, I try to describe true modesty, sister of hygiene, and daughter of gymnastics and music.

4 February 1922

The Art of Being Healthy

Even-temperedness does not generally receive external rewards; but it is certainly conducive to good health. A happy man lets himself be forgotten; glory will come to seek him out forty years after his death. But happiness is the best defense against illness, which is more intimate than envy and much more dangerous. The sad man retorts in disagreement that happiness is an effect and not a cause; that is too simplistic. Strength leads to a liking for gymnastics; but gymnastics, willingly practiced, gives us strength. In short, there is certainly a visceral posture, if I may use the expression, which favors combat and elimination, and another, quite the opposite, which constricts and poisons the person who assumes it. No doubt we cannot stretch and massage our own viscera as we can stretch out our fingers; but since joy is the obvious sign of good visceral posture, we can wager that all thoughts which lead to joy are conducive to good health as well.

Should we then rejoice when we are ill? But, you say, that is absurd and impossible. Wait a moment. It has been frequently said that the life of a soldier, except for the projectiles, is good for the health. I was able to find that out for myself, having for three years led the life of a wild rabbit who makes three little forays through the dew, and runs back into his hole at the slightest sound. Three years without feeling anything but fatigue and the need to sleep. And yet, I had been afflicted with the sickness of my time and, since the age of twenty, had suffered from a mortal malady, like all those who think without acting. One can easily say that my flourishing health during those three years was due to the country air and an active life; but I perceive other causes. An infantry corporal, the same one who once said to me, "We're not afraid any more; we're just permanently terrified," came over to my dugout one day, his face beaming with happiness. "For once," he said, "I'm really sick. I've got a fever; the major told me so; I'm going to see him again tomorrow. Maybe it's typhoid; I can't even stand up any more; everything is whirling around. They'll send me to the hospital. After two and a half years of mud, it's about time I had a little luck." But I could see very well that his joy was curing him. The next day there was no fever; instead, he crossed the lovely ruins of the Battle of Flirey to take up a position that was even worse than the one he left.

It is not a sin to be ill; discipline can say nothing to the contrary, nor can honor. What soldier has not continually searched within himself, hoping fervently to discern symptoms of an illness, even a mortal illness? During those horrible days, one ends up thinking that it would be very pleasant to die from an illness. Such thoughts are most effective in preventing all illnesses. Joy disposes the body to health better than the most skillful doctor could. There is no longer any fear of being ill, which always worsens health. If, as is said, there were indeed hermits who waited for death which, in their eyes, was a grace from God, I would not be surprised if they lived to be a hundred. The longevity which we admire in old people, when they have ceased taking an interest in anything, is no doubt due to the fact that they no longer have any fear of dying. It is always good to understand these things, as it is good to understand that it is stiffness, resulting from fear, which makes the horseman fall. There is a kind of insouciance that is a great and powerful ruse.

28 September 1921

Victories

As soon as a man looks for happiness, it is certain that he will not find it, and there is no mystery about this. Happiness is not like an object that you see in a store window and decide to buy, pay for, and carry away; if you looked at it carefully, then afterwards when you get it home, it will be blue or red, just as it was in the store window. Whereas happiness is happiness only when you yourself actually have it; if you look for it out in the world, outside of yourself, nothing will ever have the appearance of happiness. In sum, we can neither debate nor predict with regard to happiness; we must have it now. When it seems to be in the future, stop and think about it, for you already have it. To hope is to be happy.

Poets often explain things badly; and I can very well understand why; they have so much difficulty arranging syllables and rhymes that they are forced to content themselves with commonplaces. They say that happiness glitters as long as it is in the distance and in the future, and that when one actually has it, it is not the least bit interesting; as if one were trying to grasp the rainbow, or hold a rushing stream in the palm of one's hand. But this is speaking crudely. It is impossible to chase after happiness, except perhaps in words; and what especially saddens those who look for happiness around them is that they cannot even really manage to want it. Playing bridge means nothing to me, because I don't play. Boxing and fencing, likewise. Music, too, can please only the person who has first overcome certain difficulties; the same for reading. It takes courage to plunge into Balzac; one is bored at first. The way a lazy reader goes about it is quite amusing; he leafs through the pages, he reads a few lines, he throws the book aside; the happiness derived from reading is so unexpected that it astonishes even an experienced reader. We do not enjoy knowledge from afar; we must enter into it. And there must be some constraint at the outset, and some difficulty at all times. Methodical work and victory after victory, that, no doubt, is the formula for happiness. And when the action is shared with others, as in a game of cards, or in music, or in war, it is then that happiness is greatest.

But there are forms of solitary happiness that always bear the same marks—action, work, victory; such is the happiness of a miser or of a collector, who are, moreover, very much alike. How do you account for the fact that miserliness is considered a vice, especially if the miser is very attached to old gold pieces, whereas we admire the man who displays his enamels, or his ivories, or his paintings, or his rare books? We make fun of a miser who is not willing to exchange his gold for other pleasures, whereas there are bibliophiles who never read their books for fear of getting them dirty. Indeed, these kinds of happiness, like all others, are impossible to enjoy from afar; it is the collector himself who likes postage stamps, and I can't understand why. Similarly, it is the boxer who likes boxing, the hunter who likes hunting, and the politician who likes politics. It is in freely chosen action that we are happy; it is through the regulations we impose upon ourselves that we are happy; in a word, through freely accepted discipline, whether in soccer or in the study of science. And these obligations, seen from afar, do not appear enjoyable, but, on the contrary, disagreeable. Happiness is a reward that comes to those who have not looked for it.

18 March 1911

Poets

There was a beautiful friendship between Goethe and Schiller, as can be seen from their letters. Each one gave the other the only assistance one man can expect from another: that his friend support him and ask only that he remain himself. It is no great accomplishment to take people as they are, and we must always do so eventually; but to wish them to be as they are, that is genuine love. These two men, then, each developing his own creative capacities, agreed at least on the fact that differences are good and that values do not range from a rose to a horse, but from a rose to a beautiful rose, and from a horse to a beautiful horse. It is often said that there is no point in arguing about tastes, and this is true if one person prefers a rose and another, a horse; but when it comes to defining a beautiful rose or a beautiful horse, there is some point in discussing it because we can come to an agreement. However, these examples, although they lead us in the right direction, are still only abstract ones, for such living things are still held in bondage by the limitations of their species, or by us and our needs. No one will dispute the merits of music or painting; but one can profitably discuss an original painting

* 237

and a copy, finding in one the signs of a natural talent developing according to its own laws, and in the other, the scars of
servitude and a development imposed by external ideas. Our
two poets surely felt these differences in the tip of their pens.
The admirable thing is that, arguing between themselves and
often discussing the nature of perfection and of the ideal,
neither ever strayed for a single moment from his own genius.
Each gives lengthy advice to the other, and it amounts to saying: "That is how I would have done it." But at the same time,
each knows how to say that what he advises will not be of use
to the other; and the other one, by way of answer, vigorously
returns the advice to the adviser, determined to find his way
by himself.

I suppose that the poet, and indeed every artist, is coun-
seled by happiness about what he can and cannot do; for happiness, as Aristotle said, is the sign of power. But, to my mind,
this rule is applicable to everyone. The only danger in the
world is a man who is bored. All those who are called wicked
are discontent because they are bored, not discontent because
they are wicked; the boredom that pursues them everywhere
is the sign that they are in no way developing their potentiali-
ties, and so they act blindly and mechanically. Moreover, the
raving madman is no doubt the only creature in the world who
expresses simultaneously the most profound unhappiness and
pure wickedness. However, in those whom we call wicked,
and in each of us as well, I discern something misguided and
mechanical together with the rage of a slave. On the other
hand, what is done in happiness is good. Works of art clearly
bear witness to this. We say with conviction that a brush
stroke is felicitous. But every good action is in itself beautiful
and shines on a man's face. It is universally true that we never
fear anything from a beautiful face. And so I surmise that per-
fections never run counter to each other, and that it is only

imperfections and vices that clash; fear is a striking example of this. And that is why chaining people up, which is the method of tyrants and cowards, has always seemed to me essentially foolish, and the source of every folly. Untie, liberate, and do not be afraid. He who is free is disarmed.

12 September 1923

Happiness Is Virtue

There is a kind of happiness that is no more a part of us than is an overcoat. Such is the happiness of inheriting or of winning a lottery; and such is glory, for it depends on circumstances. But the happiness that depends on our own capabilities is, on the contrary, an integral part of us; it colors us more profoundly than crimson colors wool. A wise man of antiquity, escaping a shipwreck and reaching the shore completely naked, said: "I bear with me my entire fortune." Thus Wagner bore his music, and Michelangelo, all the sublime figures that he would draw. The boxer, too, has his fists and his legs and all the fruit of his work, and this is different from wearing a crown or having money. However, there are several ways of having money, and he who knows how to make money, as they say, is still rich in himself at the very moment he has lost everything.

The wise men of former times strove to find happiness; not their neighbor's happiness, but their own happiness. The wise men of today all agree that one's own happiness is not a noble thing to strive for; some of them make a point of saying that virtue scorns happiness, and this is not hard to say; others teach that the happiness of everyone is the true source of the individual's happiness, which is no doubt the emptiest idea of them all; for there is no activity more futile than pouring happiness into people around you, as if into leaky flasks; I have observed that you cannot amuse people who are bored with themselves; and that, on the contrary, you can give something to those who do not beg; for example, music to him who has become a musician. In short, nothing is to be gained from sowing in the sand; and after thinking about it carefully, I believe that I have understood the famous parabole of the sower who considered those lacking in everything unworthy of receiving anything. He who is powerful and happy through himself will then be even happier and more powerful through others. Yes, the happy will have a lively trade and will get much for what they give; but still, they must have happiness within them in order to be able to give it. And the determined man should take a good look at that concept, which will turn him away from liking what is useless.

My opinion, then, is that intimate and private happiness is not contrary to virtue, but rather is itself a virtue, as that beautiful word suggests to us, since virtue means strength. For the man who is happiest, in the true sense of the word, is clearly the one who will most easily throw the other kind of happiness overboard, just as one discards a garment. But his true wealth he does not discard, and he cannot; nor can the infantryman who attacks, nor the pilot whose plane is going down; their intimate happiness is as securely attached to them as their own life; they fight using their happiness as if it were a weapon; which has prompted some people to say that a dying hero is filled with happiness. But here we must correct the image by means of the kind of formula characteristic of Spinoza, and say: It is not because they died for their country that they were happy, but, on the contrary, it is because they were happy that they had the strength to die. Let this be woven into the memorial wreaths of November.

5 November 1922

Happiness Is Generous

We must will to be happy, and work at it. If we remain in the position of an impartial observer, simply waiting for happiness and leaving the doors open so that it can come in, it is sadness that will enter. Pessimism is true to the extent that a bit of un-controlled ill humor suits the sad man and the angry man; which may be seen in a child who has nothing to do, and we need not wait very long to witness it. The attraction of play-ing, so strong at that age, is not like the attraction of a piece of fruit that arouses hunger or thirst; rather, I see in it the will to be happy by playing, just as others are seen to be happy in their games. And here the will can get hold of something, because it is only a matter of moving about, of spinning a top, of running and shouting—things that one can will, because they can be immediately performed. The same determination may be seen in social pleasures, which are pleasures by decree, but which still require that you put yourself into them by assuming the proper attire and manners; and this sustains the decree. What the city dweller especially likes about the coun-try is the going there; action carries within it the object de-sired. I believe that it is impossible for us really to desire what we cannot do, and that hope, when unassisted by effort, is always sad. That is why our private life is always sad if we simply wait for happiness like something that is our due.

Each of us has seen some family tyrant; and we tend to think simplistically that an egoist makes of his own temperament the law he imposes on those around him; but that is not the way things are; the egoist is sad because he is waiting for happiness; even if he should be free of the little ills of life which are scarcely ever absent, boredom sets in; thus, it is the law of boredom and unhappiness which the egoist imposes on those who love or fear him. In contrast, good humor has something generous about it; it gives rather than receives. It is very true that we ought to think of the happiness of others; but it is not often enough said that the best thing we can do for those who love us is to be happy ourselves.

That is what politeness teaches us, for it is a semblance of happiness that is quickly felt through the effect which external forces have on internal forces—a law that is constant, and constantly forgotten; thus polite people are quickly rewarded, without realizing that they are being rewarded. The most flattering mark of respect one can receive from young people, and which never fails to impress, is that, in the presence of older people, they do not lose the bloom of happiness which is beauty; it is like a grace that they bestow; and we apply the word grace, in one of the other meanings of this word so rich in meanings, to that happiness which is without cause, which comes from the fount of being as from a spring. In graciousness there is a little more attention, and also intention; this is what follows when the riches of youth are no longer sufficient. But whoever the tyrant may be, one may always pay him court by eating well and by appearing not to be bored. That is why a tyrant who is sad and who seems to dislike the joy of others is often vanquished and overcome by those in whom joy is stronger than any other force. Authors, too, are enjoyable because of their joy in writing, and we very appropriately speak of felicity of expression, a happy turn of phrase. Every embellishment comes from joy. Other people never ask anything from us except what we ourselves consider to be most pleasurable. Therefore, politeness has been called the art of living.

10 April 1923

The Art of Being Happy

Children really ought to be taught the art of being happy. Not the art of being happy when misfortune strikes; I'll leave that to the Stoics; but the art of being happy when things are tolerable and life's bitterness is reduced to little annoyances and minor discomforts.

The first rule would be never to talk to others about one's own misfortunes, present or past. It ought to be considered impolite to describe to others in even the most delicate terms a headache, an upset stomach, an attack of heartburn or indigestion. The same holds true for injustices and disappointments. One ought to explain to children and young people, adults too, something they forget all too often it seems to me: that complaining can only sadden others, that is to say, eventually become unpleasant even to those who seem to invite confidences, even to those who seem to want to give consolation. For sadness is like something poisonous; one can like it, but it can only be harmful to us; and it is always the strongest feeling which finally wins out. Everyone seeks to live, not to die; and everyone seeks out the living—by that I mean those who say they are happy, and who appear happy. What a marvelous thing human society would be if everyone put his wood on the fire instead of sniveling over the ashes!

Note that these rules were formerly those of polite society; and it is true that people became bored because of not being able to speak freely. Our bourgeoisie has managed to introduce into small talk all the candor one could want; and that is a good thing. However, it is hardly a reason for each person to add his miseries to the lot; it would only make for greater boredom. And it is a reason for enlarging one's society beyond the family; for often in the family circle, because of either too much self-abandon or too much security, people come to complain about little things they would not even think of if they were in the least concerned with being agreeable. The satisfaction of being involved in high-level dealings probably results from the fact that one is forced to disregard many minor annoyances too boring to talk about. A man thus involved takes pains, as they say, to further his interests, and these pains, like those of a musician or a painter, turn into pleasure; but he is first of all freed from all the little pains that he has neither the opportunity nor the time to discuss. This is the principle involved: if you do not talk about your pains, I mean your little pains, you will not think about them for very long.

In this art of being happy which I am proposing, I should also include some practical advice about making good use of bad weather. At the moment I am writing this, it is raining; there is a patter on the roof; hundreds of little rills are chattering; the air is clean, almost filtered; the storm clouds are like strips of magnificent cloth. One must learn to seize such beauties. "But," someone says, "rain ruins the harvest." Another complains: "Mud makes everything dirty." And still a third: "It's so nice to be able to sit on the grass." Of course, everyone feels the same way; but your complaining does no good; and I get inundated with complaints that follow me even into my own home. Especially in rainy weather one wants to see smiling faces. So, show a happy face in bad weather.

8 September 1910

The Obligation to Be Happy

It is not difficult to be unhappy or discontented; all you have to do is sit down, like a prince waiting to be amused; this attitude of lying in wait and weighing happiness as if it were a commodity casts the gray shadow of boredom over everything; it is not without its majesty, for there is a kind of power involved in scorning all offerings; but in this attitude I also perceive impatience and anger directed against those ingenious workers who create their happiness out of almost nothing, like children who make castles out of sand. I flee. Experience has clearly shown me that people who are bored with themselves cannot be distracted.

Happiness, on the other hand, is a beautiful thing to see; in fact, there is nothing more beautiful. What could be more beautiful than a child? He throws himself wholeheartedly into his games; he does not wait for someone to amuse him. It is true that a pouting child shows us the other side of the coin, the refusal of all joy; fortunately, children forget quickly, but each of us has no doubt known grown-up children who have never stopped pouting. I realize that they may have good reasons; it is always difficult to be happy; happiness is a constant struggle against many events and many people; one might possibly be vanquished; it is certain that there are insurmountable obstacles and misfortunes which are stronger than the apprentice in stoicism; but our clearest obligation is to fight with all our strength before considering ourselves vanquished. Above all, and this seems quite apparent to me, it is impossible to be happy if one does not have the desire to be happy; one must therefore will one's happiness, and create it.

What has not been sufficiently stressed is that we also have an obligation toward others to be happy. It is often said that only the happy are loved; but it is forgotten that this recompense is just and deserved; for unhappiness, boredom, and despair are in the air we all breathe; and so we owe thanks and a laurel wreath to those who dissipate the miasmas and, in a sense, purify life around us with their energetic example. There is indeed nothing more profound in love than the vow to be happy. What can be more difficult to overcome than the boredom, sadness, or unhappiness of those we love? Every man and every woman should always keep in mind the fact that happiness—I mean the happiness one conquers for oneself—is the most beautiful and the most generous gift one can give.

I would even go so far as to propose a public honor to reward those men who have resolutely chosen happiness. For, in my opinion, all those corpses, all that destruction, those fantastic expenditures, and those precautionary offensives are the work of men who have never known how to be happy and who cannot tolerate others who are trying to be. As a boy, I was one of those heavyweights who are hard to defeat, hard to get moving, and slow to get excited. So it often happened that some featherweight, skinny from sadness and boredom, thought it was fun to pull my hair, pinch and tease me, until I would give him a good, solid punch, which put an end to it all. Nowadays, when I spot some gnome who announces imminent war and paves the way for it, I never listen to his arguments, because I know all about those malicious demons who cannot bear to see others living peacefully. Thus, peaceful France and peaceful Germany seem to me to be robust children, pestered and finally exasperated beyond endurance by a mere handful of spiteful boys.

16 March 1923

XCIII

One Must Vow

Pessimism comes from our passions; optimism from the will. Every man who simply lets himself go is sad; but sad is not a strong enough word, for soon he becomes angry and enraged. Similarly, we can see that children's games, if they are without rules, turn into fights; and for no other reason than the fact that uncontrolled energy always claws at itself. When you come down to it, there are no good passions; passions, correctly speaking, are always bad, and all happiness comes from the will and from self-control. In both cases, reasoning is but a servant. Our passions create astonishing systems, which we see in an exaggerated form in the case of madmen; there is always verisimilitude and eloquence in the words of an unhappy man who believes that he is persecuted. Optimistic eloquence is of a kind that calms; it takes the offensive only against garrulous rage; it soothes; the tone is what convinces, and the words are less important than the melody. The doglike growling, which can always be heard in our passions, is the first thing that must be amended; for it is a malady within us, and it produces all sorts of maladies outside us. That is

250 *

Either put yourself into it, or don't do it at all, following the lessons of our experiences which indicate that all uncontrolled thoughts are false. This energetic decision reduces all such thoughts to the level of dreams, and paves the way for those happy dreams that have no thorns. Conversely, the key that opens the door to daydreams makes us attach importance to everything. It is the key to unhappiness.

29 September 1923

why politeness is a good rule in politics; the two words are related; he who is polite is politic.

Insomnia can teach us something here; and we are all familiar with this singular affliction which can lead us to believe that existence itself is unbearable. But we must take a closer look. Self-control is part of our existence; better, it directs and makes secure our existence. First of all, through action. The thoughts of a man who is sawing wood soon work to his own benefit. When the pack is out hunting, the dogs do not fight among themselves. Thus the first remedy for the ills of thought is to saw wood. But thought that is thoroughly awakened is in itself calming; by making a choice, it clears the air. To return to the malady of insomnia: you want to sleep, and you command yourself to refrain from moving or making a choice. In this absence of control, soon both your movements and your ideas are proceeding along a mechanical track; the dogs start fighting. Every movement is convulsive, and every thought is biting. You begin to have doubts about your best friend; all signs are interpreted unfavorably; in your own eyes, you seem ridiculous and stupid. These images are very strong, and it is not the hour to go out and saw wood.

This shows very plainly that optimism requires an oath. However strange it may seem at first, we must vow to be happy. The master's whip must put a stop to the dogs' howling. Finally, as a precaution, every sad thought must be deemed false. This is necessary, because we create unhappiness quite naturally as soon as we do nothing. Boredom proves it. But the best proof that our thoughts are not in themselves biting, and that it is our own agitation that irritates us, is the happy state of somnolence in which the whole body is relaxed; such a state does not last; when we feel like this, sleep is not far off. The art of sleeping, which can help nature along, consists principally in refusing to indulge in half-thoughts.